Knitting Now

Knitting Now

Gabi Tubbs

Charles Scribner's Sons
New York

**Library of Congress Cataloging in
Publication Data**

Tubbs, Gabi.
  Knitting now.

  1. Knitting—Patterns. I. Title
TT820.T83 1985   746.9′2   84-27701
ISBN 0-684-18379-X (pbk.)

First impression 1985

 Produced in association with
Tigerlily Ltd
34 Marshall Street
London W1

Colour Photography by Belinda Banks
Designed by Anthony Lawrence and Hilly Beavan

Filmset by Advanced Filmsetters (Glasgow) Ltd
Printed and bound in Italy by
New Interlitho, S.p.a. Milan

Contents

Introduction

Knitting fabric is built up by looping a thread between two needles, thereby interlocking it as the work is transferred back and forth from one needle to the other. Whether the result is a plain smooth "cloth", an elaborately cabled fisherman's sweater or a gossamer lace shawl fine enough to be slipped through a wedding ring, only two basic stitches are used. These are the *knit* stitch and the *purl* stitch, and it is the juxtaposition of the two, following pattern instructions, plus the type of thread and the diameter of the knitting needles that determine the result.

TEXTURE

Textural patterns vary from the very simple ones described below to the more intricate basketweaves, bobbles, laces and "tweeds" which are illustrated further on.

Garter stitch is the simplest. Made using the knit stitch exclusively, row after row. The result is a series of horizontal ridges rather like a ploughed field with almost no furrow showing.

Stocking or stockinette stitch with its flat interlocking plaited effect is the most familiar of all knitting textures and is produced by alternately "knitting" one row and "purling" the next. Reverse stocking stitch has the purled or rough side of the fabric as the finished or "right" side.

Ribbing is most often used to edge sweaters. It is made by alternating one (or two) knit stitches with the same number of purl ones, building up vertical corrugated ridges.

Moss or seed stitch, a variation of ribbing, gives a "seeded" texture. First a row of single rib is knitted, then, in subsequent rows, a knit stitch is placed above a purl one and a purl stitch above a knitted one.

TENSION/GAUGE

This refers to the number of stitches and the number of rows it takes to knit a given measurement, in this case 10 cm or 4″ square, using the size of needles, type of yarn and stitch called for in the pattern. Should the tension square measure less than that stated in the pattern, it means you are working too tightly and the garment will be too small. Change to a size larger needle and test again. Equally, if your test square is too large, try using a smaller needle. It is crucially important to get the tension right because the effect of a small variation will be cumulative.

MATERIALS

In addition to knitting needles and yarn, a pair of scissors, a tape measure, and a small ruler (for measuring tension/gauge squares) are needed.

Needles. Correct needle size is most important since the diameter of the needle affects stitch size and, consequently, the overall size. The needle chart lists needle sizes and their equivalent sizes for foreign-made needles. Each pattern states both the metric and the USA needle size.

Yarn. The patterns in this book *recommend* specific brand name yarns. At the back of the book is a list of the yarn distributors and their addresses, but where there is difficulty obtaining a specific yarn locally, an equivalent must be chosen. To facilitate this, weight and length are given of the yarns used in each pattern.

When buying knitting yarn, a sufficient supply must be purchased to complete the pattern, because dye lots differ and the same yarn bought later on may be marginally

KNITTING NEEDLE CONVERSION TABLE

US SIZES	METRIC SIZES	OLD UK SIZES
0	2 mm	14
1	2¼ mm	13
	2½ mm	
2	2¾ mm	12
	3 mm	11
3	3¼ mm	10
4	3½ mm	
5	3¾ mm	9
	4 mm	8
6		
7	4½ mm	7
8	5 mm	6
9	5½ mm	5
10	6 mm	4
10½	6½ mm	3
	7 mm	2
	7½ mm	1
11	8 mm	0
13	9 mm	00
15	10 mm	000

different in colour. The dye lot of a yarn is always printed on its wrapper, and it is always worth checking to see that all balls have the same dye lot number on them.

YARN SUBSTITUTION
When substituting another yarn for the one recommended in a pattern, make absolutely sure that it corresponds in weight and thickness. Test it by knitting a tension/gauge square before beginning to work the pattern. It may be necessary to adjust the needle size to get the right measurement. Also, if the equivalent yarn is a different length from that of the recommended brand name, this must be taken into account.

Knitting yarns are referred to in many different and imprecise ways, which can be misleading. However, the following terms are in general use to describe different weights or thicknesses of ordinary wools, beginning with the finer grades:

2ply or 3ply (UK)/fingering yarn (USA)

4ply (UK)/fingering to sport yarn (USA)

double knitting (UK)/sport to knitting worsted yarn (USA)

chunky (UK)/bulky (USA)

extra chunky (UK)/extra bulky (USA)

Other fibres such as bouclé or cotton, mohair, angora or chenille are normally described in one of four weights – light weight, medium weight, chunky/bulky or extra chunky/bulky.

READING A PATTERN
Knitting patterns contain detailed stitch-by-stitch instructions set out according to certain developed conventions, such as the use of abbreviations. See opposite.

Sizes. When instructions give different sizes, the smallest size is given first: the subsequent ones are in parentheses, i.e. 32 (34, 36, 38). The knitter must of course follow instructions for one size throughout the pattern, and relevant instructions will fall in the same place as the size number, so that k3 (4, 5, 6) would mean to knit 3 stitches for size 32, 4 stitches for size 34, and so on. Where there is only one set of figures, it applies to all sizes.

Measurements are given throughout both in metric and inches.

Special terms
Knitwise (purlwise). Insert needle into the next stitch as if about to knit (purl).

Pick up and knit (purl). Knit (purl) into the loops alongside edge of fabric, as when beginning a neckline.

UK/USA TERMINOLOGY
In the United Kingdom and the USA most knitting terms are the same. *Where they are different the UK term is given first.* For example, cast/bind off. The size of knitting needles (see chart) and the general description of yarns (see Yarns) are also different.

READING COLOUR CHARTS
Colour charts are another method of stitch-by-stitch instructions, used when more than one colour is being worked, for instance in Fair-isle designs or multi-coloured motifs.

Colour charts are presented on graphs. Each square represents one stitch. When charts are printed in black and white, the colour is coded: for example, X for green, O for yellow, and so on. Examples on pages 11 and 82.

HOW TO KNIT
Illustrated instructions over-leaf show how to cast stitches on to the needle in order to begin work, how to make knit and purl stitches, and increase and decrease the number of stitches on a needle so that work becomes either narrower or broader; finally, how to bind/cast off when a piece is finished. With this information, it is possible to knit any of the patterns in this book.

Attaching new yarn. Never tie a new thread on in the middle of a piece of work. It will probably show. Instead, join at the outer edge of work. Make a slip knot with the new strand around the working strand, then move the slip knot up to the edge of the work and continue knitting.

Changing to a new colour. To prevent holes when working in two or more colours, pick up the new colour from underneath the dropped strand.

ASSEMBLY
Blocking and steaming. Before pieces are sewn together it is often possible to adjust their shape and dimensions slightly by blocking and steaming. Pin each piece to a padded surface such as an ironing board. Use plenty of pins close together to avoid ruffled edges.

Joining pieces. To prevent splitting yarn, use a blunt needle to sew the pieces together. Use either a thread of knitting yarn, or, in the case of bulky yarns, separate the strands and use one of them. The methods of stitching are illustrated overleaf.

ABBREVIATIONS
alt   alternate
approx   approximately
beg   begin(ning)
ch   chain(s)
cm   centimetre(s)
cn   cable needle
cont   continu(e)(ing)
dc   double crochet (US: sc)
dec   decreas(e)(ing)
dpn   double-pointed needles
foll   follow(ing)
g   gramme(s)
g st   garter stitch
inc   increas(e)(ing)
k   knit
LH   left hand
m   metre(s)
mm   millimetre(s)
No   number
oz   ounce(s)
p   purl
patt   pattern
psso   pass slip stitch(es) over
rem   remain(s)(ing)
rep   repeat(ing)
RH   right hand
RS   right side
sc   single crochet (UK: dc)
sl   slip
sl st   slip stitch (UK: crochet – ss)
ss   slip stitch (US: crochet – sl st)
st(s)   stitch(es)
st st   stocking stitch (US: stockinette st)
tbl   through back loop(s)
tog   together
WS   wrong side
yd   yard(s)
yfwd   yarn forward (US: yo)
yo   yarn over needle (UK: yfwd, yon, yrn)
yon   yarn over needle (US: yo)
yrn   yarn round needle (US: yo)
[]   repeat instructions inside brackets as many times as indicated
*   repeat instructions following * as many times as indicated

Make a slip loop on left-hand needle (1).

Insert right-hand needle into slip loop from front to back and wind yarn under and over the point of right-hand needle (2).

Draw right-hand needle and yarn forward through slip loop (3).

Transfer the loop now on right-hand needle to left-hand needle.

Insert right-hand needle between two loops now on left-hand needle (4).

Wind yarn under and over the point of right-hand needle, as in (2) and draw loop through (3).

Transfer new loop over to left-hand needle as before and continue.

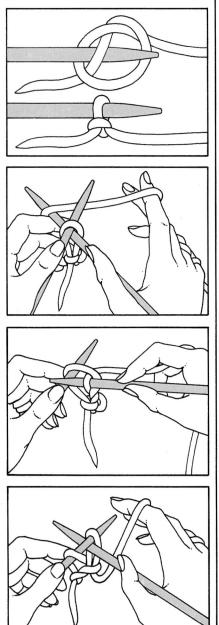

Thumb method of casting on

Make a slip knot (fig. 1 opposite) about 1 yd/metre from end of yarn. This counts as first stitch.

Hold needle in right hand and *shorter* end of yarn in left-hand, securing against palm as shown (1).

Insert needle under secured yarn, then wind yarn from main ball under and over the point of the needle (2) and draw the needle towards you and through the loop on thumb (3). This makes the next stitch (4).

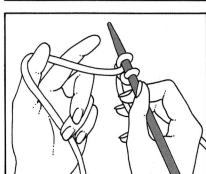

Knit Stitch

Hold needle with cast-on stitches in left hand. Insert right-hand needle from front to back into first stitch (1). Loop yarn round point of needle (2) from behind.

Draw right-hand needle forward through cast-on stitch (3). Pull right-hand needle to right to slip off old stitch (4), leaving new stitch on right-hand needle.

Repeat these steps with every cast-on stitch, to complete one row.

To knit next row, swap needles so that knitting is in left hand and continue as above.

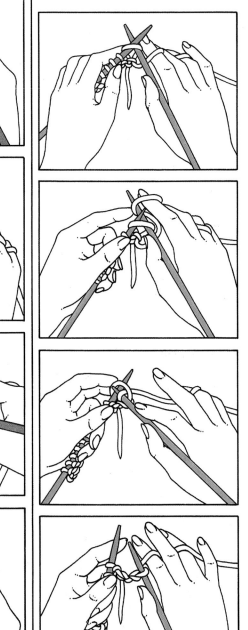

Keep yarn in front. Slip needle into stitch *from behind*, looping yarn round needle (1), and draw it through stitch now on both needles to right needle (2). Old stitch slips off left needle (3).

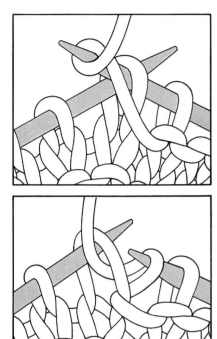

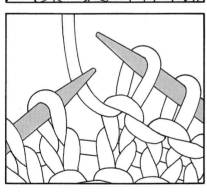

Decreasing

Two methods: pattern instructions will say which to use. Knit or purl two stitches together by slipping the left-hand needle into two instead of only one stitch (abbreviation: *K2 tog*), or (p2 tog). (fig. 1).

Alternatively: *sl 1, k1, psso* (fig. 2). Slip one stitch from left to right needle without knitting: *sl 1*.

Then knit one stitch: *k1*.

Pass the slipped stitch over the knitted stitch: *psso*.

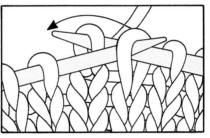

Assembly

Back stitch. Work as in sewing. Work either one stitch or a half stitch from edge.

Invisible seam. Fig. 1 shows right side.

Increasing

Knit a stitch as usual, but do not slip old stitch off the needle. Then knit a second stitch into the *back* of the stitch (1) and slip off old stitch. Space increases evenly throughout work.

To increase at beginning or end of a row, simply loop yarn round needle point (2).

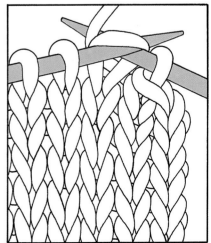

Casting/ binding off

Knit two stitches loosely. Then, using the tip of the left-hand needle, slip the first stitch over the second (1).

Knit another stitch loosely (2) and slip previous stitch over it. Continue to last stitch but one, break yarn and draw end back through last stitch.

NB Always cast/bind off in the pattern worked. To cast/bind off ribbing, knit the knit stitches and purl the purl stitches.

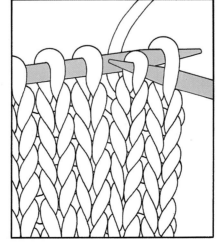

Modern Times

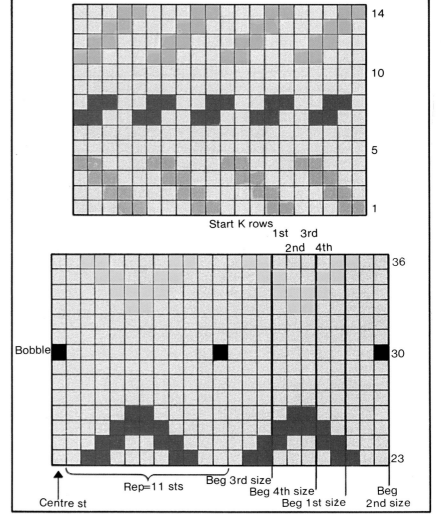

14

10

5

1

Start K rows

1st 3rd
2nd 4th

36

Bobble

30

23

Rep=11 sts

Beg 3rd size

Centre st

Beg 4th size

Beg 1st size

Beg 2nd size

Cable Sweater, knitted in royal blue, combines a simple raglan sleeved shape with a cable, leaf and raised stripe pattern on plain reversed stocking stitch background.

Dots and Dashes (far right). Brilliant Fairisle and bobble pattern contrast with the sand-coloured stocking stitch base of this easy shirt shape. The chart gives stitch-by-stitch instructions for placement of colour.

Patterns on pages 62 and 63.

Batty Blue

Fluid shape batwing cardigan in fine yarn nips neatly into the waist. An all-over eyelet pattern and a feminine ruffled collar edged in heather and black add softness to this generously-styled shape. *Pattern on page 63.*

Romantic Whites

Soft Lace (left) is a delicate, open honeycomb-stitch pattern knitted into a loose blouse style with raglan sleeves and a wide drawstring neckline. Back view below.

Frothy Lace (centre). This easy, basic design is enhanced by mixing a romantic lace pattern with a soft, snow-white mohair yarn.

Frilled Top (right). Elegant cap sleeved, languid shape with frilled, revealing neckline is very easy to knit. Pretty buttons fasten at shoulder, and delicate beads and crystals embellish an unfussy stitch pattern.

Patterns on pages 64 and 65.

Cassata Waistcoat

Natural dishcloth cotton sets off strong pastel stripes in mercerised cotton, and creates an interesting texture for this otherwise classic waistcoat style. It can be knitted in men's sizes too.
Pattern on page 66.

Spun Silver

Combine a dazzling lurex yarn with an easy but effective basket-weave stitch and knit a luxurious evening top with a drawstring waist and sleeves that can be gathered at the wrist or simply turned up. A gathered wisp of gold lace softens the slashed neckline. *Pattern on page 67.*

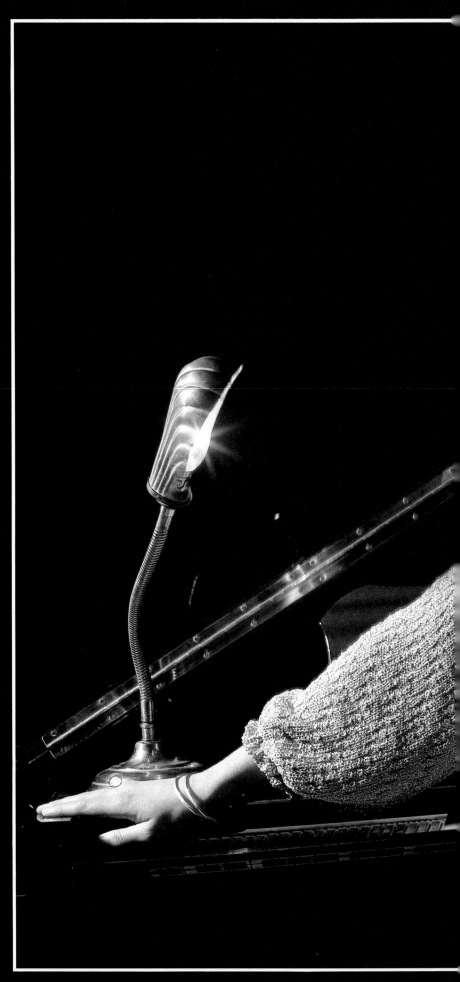

A Bigger Splash

David Hockney's famous picture inspired this sporty raglan shape knitted in single-sided fisherman's rib using a brilliantly coloured mat cotton. A modern classic to wear all year round.
Pattern on page 67.

Motorbiking

Abstract two-tone graphic pattern in a shiny, loopy yarn shapes into a loose comfortable sweater with deep armholes and an open shirt neck. Stunningly co-ordinated with a flared mini-skirt in contrasting mat black with a snug fitting ribbed yoke.
Pattern on page 68.

Gold & Black

Blend fine cotton, silky, slubbed
cotton and fluffy mohair, and, with
large needles, knit an open-
textured fabric into the easiest
dolman shape.
Pattern on page 69.

Shocking Pink

Strikingly different use of colour on front and back demands a double take. The design knits up easily in stocking stitch with the help of a chart that shows exactly when to change yarn colour. *Pattern on pages 70–73.*

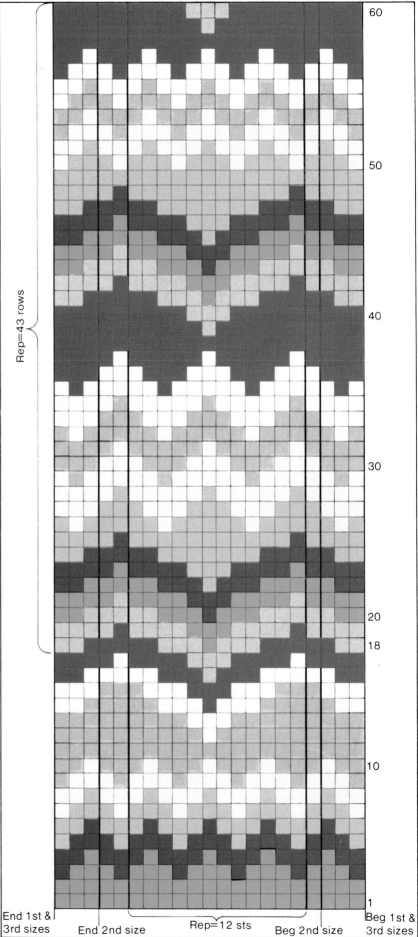

Bargello. Similar to bargello tapestry, this sharp zig-zag pattern suggests the colour spectrum of the aurora borealis. In softest mohair, with dropped shoulder and a V-neck, it remains undeniably classic in design. On the chart opposite, each square represents one stitch.
Pattern on page 74.

Earth Tints

Subtle Textures (left). Mixing a variety of yarns and stitches creates an interesting and firm fabric. Bitter chocolate base colour is lifted with bands of powder pink, black and chalk. Detail below.

Pebble (centre). Roomy, casual shirt shape with an all-over bobble grid pattern decorating a plain stocking stitch surface. It has a garter stitch shirt collar with low front buttoning tab that will look good on him too.

Lace (right). Sporty yarn and earthy tone contrast with delicate twelve-row repeat lace pattern that is easier to knit than it looks.

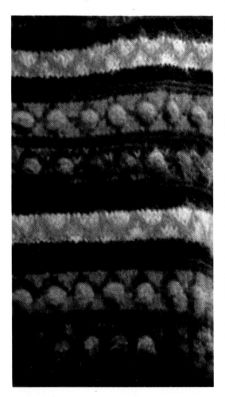

Coconut

Ideal for beginners. Feminine top with slightly puffed sleeves is knitted in stocking stitch using an unusual, fine loopy yarn with a shaggy finish. The perfect cover up for the odd mistake.
Pattern on page 77.

Oats

Very comfortable, very roomy – a diamond stitch pattern and an asymmetrical collar that buttons to make a roll neck if preferred. A step in the right direction for the not so experienced.
Pattern on page 78.

College Girls

Ribbed Sweater (left). Soft and comfortable shape, the twisted rib makes an elastic fabric, the toning mohair bands add interest.

Fairisle Slipover (centre). Here a cream base is sparked up with bands of bilberry, duckegg blue, yellow, red and sage green. To make the pattern more intricate, swiss darn/ duplicate stitch the Fairisle pattern with dashing mohair colours.

Soft Diamonds (right) form an all-over pattern mixing strong and soft pastels on pale sage ground, in mohair.

Patterns on pages 79 and 80.

His & Hers

V-neck Sweaters (left) are an adaptation of traditional Aran, updated in style and texture with dropped shoulders and deep armholes, in mercerised cotton; sizes are for both of you.

Fairisle Cardigan and **Victorian Shawl.** Combine rich midnight blue with contrasting flashes of Fairisle into a raglan sleeved, V-necked cardigan and knit a quick cover-up in mohair yarn for summer or winter.

Patterns on pages 81–83.

Bedjacket

Pure luxury for lazy mornings and cosy nights, sitting up in bed or lounging around. Delicately coloured mohair in a dainty butterfly pattern and cardigan shape that could be adapted in fashion colours for everyday wear.
Pattern on page 83.

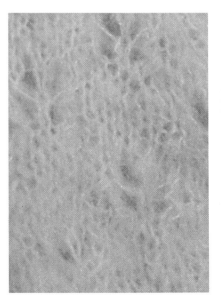

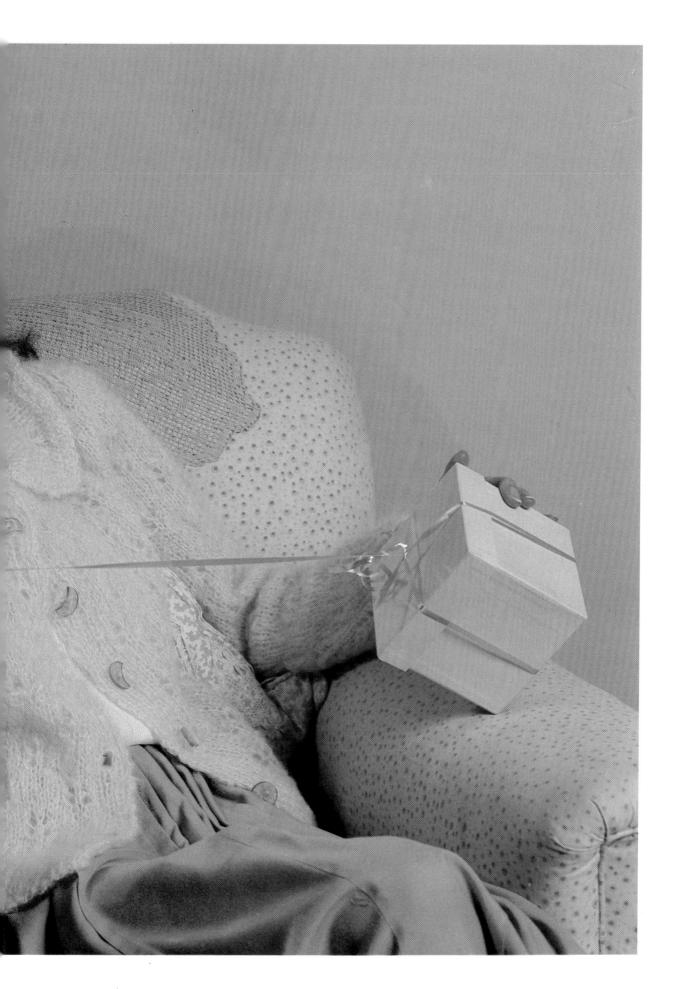

Shades of Autumn

Bold Stripes (far left) knit up swiftly in wide bands of rib, moss/seed stitch and garter stitch. The long, sporty pullover is light and easy to wear, with an unfussy neckline that sits neatly and buttons at the shoulder.

Rust Bobbles (centre). 40's inspired cardigan with gathered sleeve heads and deep V-neckline, has a blousy bodice that nips into the waist. Masses of bobbles exaggerate the yoke; the rest of the bodice and sleeves are in understated moss/seed stitch.

Yellow Leaves (right) form a deep, yoke pattern. Generously shaped sweater in matt cotton is enhanced by soft, rich yellow and a textured stitch that produces a light but firm fabric.

Patterns on pages 84–86.

Kids' Stuff

Pussycat mohair cardigan knits up quickly in stocking stitch. The unusual colour combination differs from the obvious, but the shape is classic, with a neat collar, set in sleeves and an adorable beanie hat. For extra child appeal, pussycat faces are Swiss darned (duplicate stitched) to both fronts. *Pattern on page 86.*

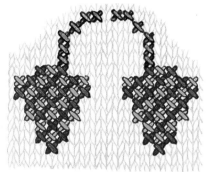

Raspberries & Cream

Easy T-shapes are the basic design feature of all three outfits. Everything including the beret is knitted using garter and stocking stitch – wonderfully simple for beginners. The yarn is machine washable. Sweet raspberries, embroidered in cross-stitch with tapestry wool, following the motif chart above, add charm.

Patterns on pages 88–90.

Country Cottage

A Country Cottage has inspired this three-dimensional picture sweater, so easy to knit using basic stitch techniques. The cottage doubles as a pocket and is stitched on separately, as are the cloud and tree. Embroider shiny red apples in satin stitch using same weight yarn. *Pattern on page 90.*

Fairisle

Just what boys like to wear. For quicker results we've used medium weight wool. The Fairisle design is uncomplicated and the stitch chart which accompanies the pattern is easily followed. It goes almost without saying, that girls look nice in it too. *Pattern on page 91.*

Sun Dress

Summer clothes have to be light and breezy, especially knitted ones. This dress in fine cotton has a lacy, gathered skirt and a snug ribbed bodice finished with delicate picot-edged straps. The same picot edging is used to decorate hem and matching socks.
Pattern on page 92.

Chequerboard

Five vivid colours combine to create an interesting geometric pattern. Straightforward crew neck sweater in soft mercerised cotton knits-up smoothly and is comfortable to wear. Embroidered names are optional: we've used chain stitch and the same yarn.
Pattern on page 93.

Red & White

Spotted Cardigan and Shorts for busy toddlers. Raglan-sleeved cardigan has a delicate surface interest created with rice stitch. The two-tone bermudas in plain knitting have plenty of give for nappies.

Frill collar Top. Roomy sweater in rich red scattered with a cream swallow pattern. The pretty Pierrot collar, swiss darned (duplicate stitched) in red to echo swallow stitch on bodice, reverses the colours to embellish the basic design.

Patterns on pages 94 and 95.

Soft Stripes

The use of colour is all important here, because it is the chief design feature of both sweaters. Vivid blue mohair (left) is softened by pastel pink cuffs, welt, collar and a bold stripe, while rich burgundy and mauve mohair create an equally dazzling effect (right). Shoulder buttoning and a round neck complete the novelty of the design, but the basic shape is the same for both sweaters.
Patterns on pages 95 and 96.

Hello, Goodbye and **Striped Sweater**.
Whether toddler or older child, let the
words and colours do the talking: the
sweater above says it for you. The easy T-
shape (far right) with garter stitch edging
and unusual stripes is definitely a begin-
ner's design. *Patterns, pages 97 and 98.*

Kids' Smocks

Lavender Blues

Adorable dress with pocket bag, neat set-in sleeves and pretty yoke detail, hangs loosely for comfort. The delicate scatter stitch in cream breaks up the base colour and also enhances the design. *Pattern on page 98.*

Patchwork Suit

All-in-one suit keeps baby snug and cosy. A zip makes changing easy and the balaclava hat tops the lot. *Pattern on page 99.*

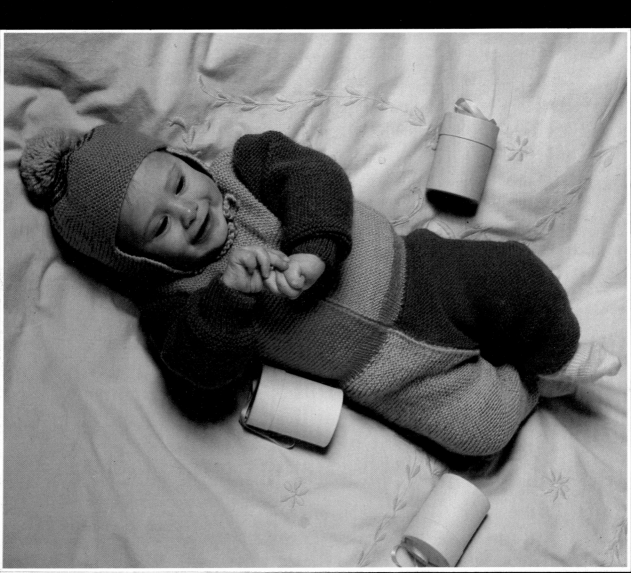

Trío

Country Sweater (far left). Sugary almond colouring combined with a nordic influenced stitch pattern knits beautifully into a little girl's favourite sweater. Neck opening allows for easy putting on and taking off.

Heather Suit (centre) for special occasions. Demure cardigan in a softly shaded and cleverly textured stitch pattern slips over gently gathered skirt with narrow plain straps and ribbed waist.

Soft Buds (right). Snug cardigan has a delicate feel because of its pretty bud pattern and use of fine mohair. The shape is roomy and long with a deep, ribbed welt.

Patterns on pages 101–103.

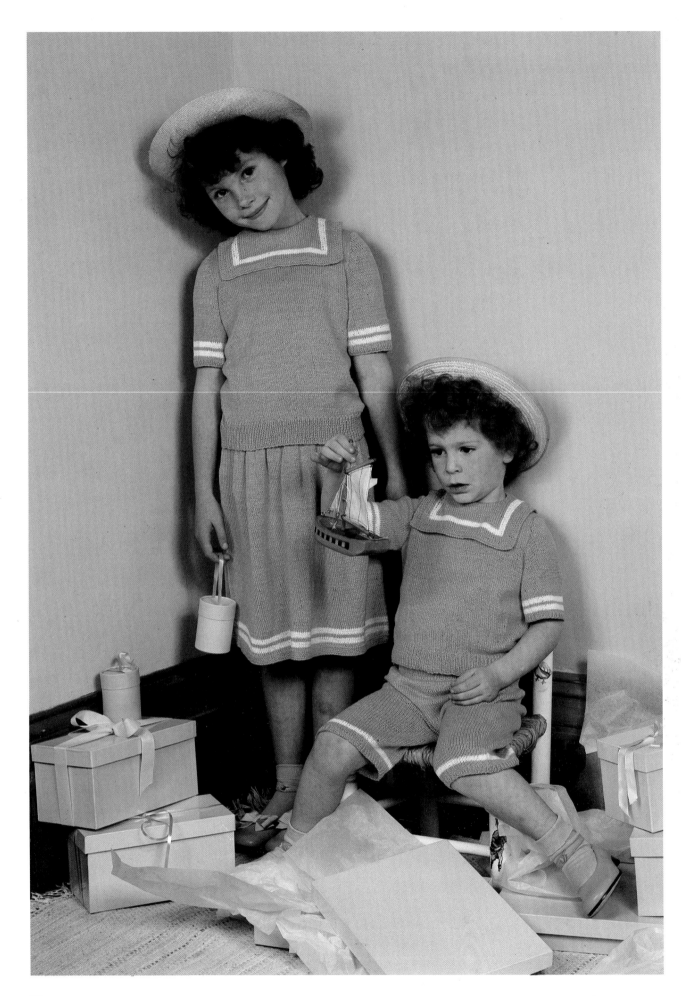

Pink & Blue

Sailor Suits (left). Pure, mercerised cotton that doesn't itch and washes like a dream. Both tops are the same shape and button at the back. Her skirt has a deep ribbed waistband; his cheeky bermudas slip on easily, yet fit snugly.
Baby Togs. Cotton bouclé sugar pink crew neck sweater has an all-over swallow pattern in blue with a snug bonnet to match. Romper pants reverse the colours with a dash of white added. Especially pretty are the delicate snowflake designs round the legs that gather into a rib at the ankles.
Patterns on pages 103–105.

FRONT

End 1st size

End 2nd size

Beg 1st size

Beg 2nd size

Palm Tree

This is what dreams are made of. Simple shape and easy stitches are
the background for this south sea island.
Pattern on page 107.

Cable Sweater

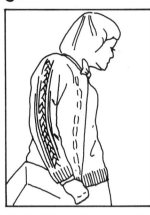

MATERIALS
9 (10, 10) 50 g/1¾ oz balls (each approx 125 m/140 yds) of Pingouin *Confort* (double knitting/sport to knitting worsted weight yarn)
1 pair each of 3¼ mm/No 3 and 4 mm/No 6 knitting needles
Set of four 3¼ mm/No 3 double-pointed knitting needles
1 cable needle

MEASUREMENTS
To fit 86 (91, 96) cm/34 (36, 38)″ bust
Length 64 (65, 66) cm/25¼ (25½, 26)″
Sleeve seam 46 cm/18″

TENSION/GAUGE
22 sts and 28 rows to 10 cm/4″ over st st using 4 mm/No 6 needles.

PLAIT PANEL (22 sts)
1st row: Knit through back loop of st (called k1b), p1, k1b, p2, k12, p2, k1b, p1, k1b.
2nd and all even numbered rows: P1b, k1, p1b, k2, p12, k2, p1b, k1, p1b.
3rd row: K1b, p1, k1b, p2, k4, sl next 4 sts on to cable needle and hold at back of work, k4, then k4 from cable needle, p2, k1b, p1, k1b.
5th row: As 1st row.
7th row: K1b, p1, k1b, p2, sl next 4 sts on to cable needle and hold at front of work, k4, then k4 from cable needle, k4, p2, k1b, p1, k1b.
8th row: As 2nd row.
Rep these 8 rows for plait panel patt.

CENTRE MOTIF PATT
(2 sts)
1st row: (RS) K twice into each st.
2nd row: P4.
3rd row: [K twice into next st, k1] twice.
4th row: P6.
5th row: K twice into first st, k3, k twice into next st, k1.
6th row: P8.
7th row: K twice into first st, k5, k twice into next st, k1.
8th row: P10.
9th row: K1, sl next 2 sts on to cable needle and hold at front of work, k2, then k2 from cable needle, sl next 2 sts on to cable needle and hold at back of work, k2, then k2 from cable needle, k1.
10th row: P1, [p2 tog 4 times, p1.
11th row: Sl 1–k1–psso, k2, k2 tog.
12th row: P2 tog, p2 tog tbl. These 12 rows form the motif. (**Note:** This is counted as 2 sts throughout.)

BACK
With smaller needles, cast on 102 (110, 114) sts.
1st row: K2, *p2, k2, rep from * to end.
2nd row: P2, *p2, k2, rep from * to end.
Rep these 2 rows for 8 cm/3¼″, ending with a WS row and inc 16 (14, 16) sts evenly across last row. 118 (124, 130) sts.
Change to larger needles and cont in patt as foll:
1st row: (RS) P4 (7, 10), *work 22 sts of plait panel, p22, rep from * once more, work 22 sts of plait panel, p4 (7, 10).
2nd row: K4 (7, 10), *work 22 sts of plait panel, k22, rep from * once more, work 22 sts of plait panel, k4 (7, 10). Cont in patt as now set until work measures 41 cm/16¼″ from beg, ending with a WS row.

Shape armholes
Keeping patt correct, cast/bind off 4 (5, 6) sts at beg of next 2 rows.
Next row: K1, p2 tog, patt to last 3 sts, p2 tog tbl, k1. back of loops (tbl), k1.
Next row: K1, k2 tog tbl, patt to last 3 sts, k2 tog, k1.
Rep last 2 rows 3 times more. 94 (98, 102) sts.
Next row: K1, p2 tog, patt to last 3 sts, p2 tog tbl, k1.
Next row: K2, patt to last 2 sts, k2.
Rep last 2 rows until 40 sts rem, ending with a RS row.
Next row: K2, patt 12, [p2 tog] 6 times, patt 12, k2.
Leave rem 34 sts on st holder.

FRONT
With smaller needles cast on 102 (110, 114) sts and work in rib as for Back for 8 cm/3¼″, ending with a WS row and inc 10 (8, 10) sts evenly across last row. 112 (118, 124) sts.
Change to larger needles and cont in patt as foll:
1st row: (RS) P4 (7, 10), patt 22 sts of plait panel, p29, k twice into each of next 2 sts, p29, patt 22 sts of plait panel, p4 (7, 10).
This sets position of centre motif. Keeping panels correct at each side, work the 2nd–12th rows of motif.
13th row: P4 (7, 10), patt 22, p12, [k twice into each of next 2 sts, p15] twice, k twice into each of next 2 sts, p12, patt 22, p4 (7, 10).
Work the 2nd–12th rows of motif over all 3 motifs, then keeping the centre plain, rep the 1st–12th rows over the motif at each side.
Rep these 36 rows 3 times more, but AT THE SAME TIME when work measures 41 cm/16¼″ from beg, ending with a WS row, shape armholes as for Back, decreasing to 48 sts (always counting centre motifs as 2 sts), ending with a WS row.

Shape neck
Next row: K1, p2 tog, patt 12, turn and leave rem sts on spare needle.
Next row: Patt to last 2 sts, k2.
Next row: K1, p2 tog, patt to last 2 sts, p2 tog tbl.
Rep last 2 rows until 4 sts rem, ending with a WS row.
Next row: P2 tog, p2 tog tbl.
Next row: K2.
P2 tog and fasten off.
Return to sts on spare needle, sl centre 18 sts on to st holder for neck, rejoin yarn and patt to last 3 sts, p2 tog tbl, k1.
Cont to match first side.

SLEEVES
With smaller needles cast on 46 (50, 54) sts and work in rib as for Back for 8 cm/3¼″, ending with a WS row and inc 10 (12, 14) sts in last row. 56 (62, 68) sts.
Change to larger needles and cont in patt as foll:

1st row: P17 (20, 23), patt 22 sts of plait panel, p to end.
Cont in patt as set, work 1 row, then inc one st at each end of next and every foll 6th row, working extra sts into reverse st st, until there are 88 (94, 100) sts, then cont without shaping until sleeve measures 46 cm/18″ from beg, ending with a WS row.

Shape top/cap
Cast/bind off 4 (5, 6) sts at beg of next 2 rows.
Next row: K1, p2 tog, patt to last 3 sts, p2 tog tbl, k1.
Next row: K2, patt to last 2 sts, k2.
Rep last 2 rows until 18 sts rem, ending with an RS row.
Next row: K2, pl, [p2 tog] 6 times, p1, k2.
Leave rem 12 sts on st holder.

NECKBAND
Join raglan seams.
With set of four double-pointed needles, k sts of right sleeve, back neck and left sleeve, knitting 2 tog at each back raglan seam, pick up and k15 sts down left front neck, k front neck sts, then pick up and k15 sts up right front neck. Work 7 rounds in k2, p2 rib.
Cast/bind off in rib.

ASSEMBLY
Join side and sleeve seams.
Press work, if necessary, according to instructions on yarn band.

Dots & Dashes

MATERIALS
7 (7, 8, 8) 50 g/$1\frac{3}{4}$ oz balls (each approx 125 m/140 yds) of Pingouin *Confort* (double knitting/sport to knitting worsted weight yarn) in main colour (M)
1 ball in each of 6 contrast colours (A, B, C, D, E and F)
1 pair each of 3 mm/No 2 and $3\frac{3}{4}$ mm/No 5 knitting needles

MEASUREMENTS
To fit 81 (86, 91, 97) cm/32 (34, 36, 38)″ bust
Length 58 (60, 62, 64) cm/$22\frac{3}{4}$ ($23\frac{1}{2}$, $24\frac{1}{2}$, $25\frac{1}{4}$)″
Sleeve seam 44 (45, 46, 47) cm/$17\frac{1}{4}$ ($17\frac{3}{4}$, 18, $18\frac{1}{2}$)″

TENSION/GAUGE
24 sts and 26 rows to 10 cm/4″ over patt using $3\frac{3}{4}$ mm/No 5 needles.
24 sts and 32 rows to 10 cm/4″ over st st $3\frac{3}{4}$ mm/ No 5 needles.

ABBREVIATIONS
MB – make bobble – [k1, p1, k1, p1, k1] all into next st, turn, p5, turn, k5, turn, p2 tog, p1, p2 tog, turn, sl 1–k2 tog–psso.

BACK
With smaller needles and M, cast on 95 (101, 107, 113) sts and work in k1, p1 rib for 8 cm/$3\frac{1}{4}$″, ending with a WS row, and inc 10 sts evenly across last row. 105 (111, 117, 123) sts.
Change to larger needles and beg with a k row, work 2 rows in st st.
Cont in st st, work patt as foll:
1st–14th rows: Work in patt foll chart I, reading odd numbered rows from right to left and even rows from left to right.
15th–22nd rows: With M, work in st st.
23rd–36th rows: Work in patt foll chart II.
37th–44th rows: With M, work in st st.
Rep 1st–44th rows to form patt, changing colours as indicated each time 44 rows are repeated.
Cont in patt until work measures 37 (38, 39, 40) cm/$14\frac{1}{2}$ (15, $15\frac{1}{4}$, $15\frac{3}{4}$)″ from beg, ending with a p row.

Shape armholes
Keeping patt correct, cast/bind off 4 sts at beg of next 2 rows, then dec one st at each end of next and every other row until 31 (33, 35, 37) sts rem, ending with a p row.
(**Note:** After patt has been worked 3 times, cont in st st using M only.)
Cast/bind off.

FRONT
Work as for Back until 47 (51, 53, 57) sts rem, ending with a p row.

Shape neck
Next row: K2 tog, k14 (16, 16, 18), turn and leave rem sts on spare needle.
Next row: P to end.
Next row: K2 tog, k to last 2 sts, k2 tog.
Rep last 2 rows 5 (6, 6, 7) times more, ending with a p row.
Next row: K2 tog, k1.
Next row: P2 tog and fasten off.
Return to sts on spare needle, cast/bind off centre 15 (15, 17, 17) sts, k to last 2 sts, k2 tog.
Cont to match first side, reversing shaping.

SLEEVES
With smaller needles and M, cast on 45 (47, 49, 51) sts and work in k1, p1 rib for 8 cm/$3\frac{1}{4}$″, ending with a WS row and inc 4 (4, 6, 6) sts in last row. 49 (51, 55, 57) sts.
Change to larger needles and beg with a k row, work 8 rows in st st, rep 23rd–44th rows of 3rd rep of patt, then beg with 1st row, cont in patt as for Back, and AT THE SAME TIME inc one st at each end of 5th and every foll 6th row until there are 79 (83, 87, 91) sts, then cont without shaping until sleeve measures approx 46 (47, 48, 49) cm/18 ($18\frac{1}{2}$, 19, $19\frac{1}{4}$)″ from beg, ending with the same patt row as at Back and Front armholes.

Shape top/cap
Dec one st at each end of next and every other row until 13 sts rem, ending with a p row.
Cast/bind off.

COLLAR
With smaller needles and M, cast on 135 (139, 143, 147) sts and work 4 rows in k1, p1 rib.
Next row: [K1, p1] twice, sl 1–k2 tog–psso, rib to last 7 sts, sl 1–k2 tog–psso, rib 4.
Work 3 rows in rib.
Rep last 4 rows 3 times more, then cast/bind off rem 119 (123, 127, 131) sts in rib.

ASSEMBLY
Press work according to instructions on yarn band.
Join raglan seams, sewing last part of sleeve seams to cast/bound off sts at armholes.
Join side and sleeve seams.
Sew on collar, beg and ending at centre front neck, then join edges of collar for approx 2 cm/$\frac{3}{4}$″.
Press seams.

Batty Blue

MATERIALS
10 (11, 12) 50 g/$1\frac{3}{4}$ oz balls (each approx 183 m/200 yds) of Lister–Lee *Motoravia 4 ply* (4 ply/fingering weight yarn) in main colour (M)
1 ball in each of 2 contrast colours (A and B)
1 pair each of $2\frac{3}{4}$ mm/No 2 and $3\frac{3}{4}$ mm/No 5 knitting needles
8 buttons

MEASUREMENTS
To fit 81 (86, 91) cm/32 (34, 36)″ bust
Length 54 (56, 58) cm/$21\frac{1}{2}$ ($22\frac{1}{4}$, 23)″

TENSION/GAUGE
30 sts and 40 rows to 10 cm/4″ over patt using $3\frac{3}{4}$ mm/No 5 needles.

PATT ST
1st–10th rows: Work 10 rows in st st, beg with a k row.
11th row: (RS) *K9, yfwd/yo, k2 tog, rep from * to end.
12th–20th rows: Work 9 rows in st st, beg with a p row.
Rep 11th–20th rows to form patt st.

BACK
With smaller needles and M,

cast on 70 (74, 78) sts.

First half

Work 40 rows in k1, p1 rib, so ending with a WS row.

Change to larger needles and beg patt, inc one st at beg of first row (sleeve edge), then inc one st at sleeve edge on every row until there are 142 (146, 150) sts.

Place marker at sleeve edge of last row to mark beg of cuff edge.

Cont in patt throughout, inc one st at sleeve edge on every other row until there are 156 (162, 168) sts.

Place marker at sleeve edge of last row to mark beg of shoulder shaping.

Shape shoulder

Beg at sleeve edge, cast/bind off 3 sts at beg of next and every foll alt row until 36 sts rem.

Cast/bind off.

Second half

Work to correspond to First half, reversing shapings.

RIGHT FRONT

With smaller needles and M, cast on 82 (86, 90) sts and work 10 rows in k1, p1 rib, so ending with a WS row.

Next row: (buttonhole row) Rib 4, yfwd/yo, k2 tog, rib to end.

Work 19 rows in rib, then work another buttonhole.

Work 9 rows in rib, sl 12 front sts on to st holder for centre front band. 70 (74, 78) sts.

Change to larger needles and work in patt, shaping side and shoulder as for Back until 138 (144, 144) sts rem.

Shape neck

Cont shoulder shaping, and AT THE SAME TIME dec one st at neck edge on next and every foll alt row 36 times in all. Fasten off.

LEFT FRONT

Work to correspond to Right Front, omitting buttonholes.

RUFFLES

(**Note:** Work 2 ruffles of each width.) With larger needles and B, cast on 140 (144, 144) sts.

K 1 row.

Using A, p 1 row, k 1 row.

Using M, work 3 rows in st st.

Next row: K, picking up loop from every 10th st of first row and knitting in tog with corresponding st on needle to form scallop.

Next row: (eyelet row) P1, *yrn/yo, p2 tog, rep from * to last st, p1.

For narrow ruffle: Work 10 rows in st st.

For medium ruffle: Work 20 rows in st st.

For wide ruffle: Work 5 rows in st st, work eyelet row as before, work 4 rows in st st, then work eyelet row as before, work 30 rows in st st.

For all ruffles: K2 tog all across next row. 70 (72, 72) sts.

Cast/bind off.

Sew centre back and shoulder seams.

With RS of sweater and ruffles facing, sew ruffles neatly around neck edge with widest ruffle underneath, then medium ruffle, then narrow ruffle on top.

SLEEVE CUFFS

With smaller needles and RS facing, pick up and k60 (66, 72) sts evenly along sleeve edge from marker to marker. Work 40 rows in k1, p1 rib. Cast/bind off in rib.

BUTTON BAND

Sl 12 sts of Left Front from st holder on to smaller needle.

With M, work in k1, p1 rib across 12 sts and cont in rib until band reaches centre back neck.

Cast/bind off in rib.

Sew band in place and mark positions of buttons, first one on 11th row from beg, the next one level with beg of front shaping, then 6 more at equal intervals.

BUTTONHOLE BAND

Work to correspond to button band, working buttonholes to correspond to positions of buttons.

Cast/bind off in rib and sew band in place.

ASSEMBLY

Join neckband seam.

Join side and sleeve seams.

Sew on buttons.

Press according to instructions on yarn band.

MATERIALS

8 (9, 9, 9) 40 g/1½ oz balls (each approx 85 m/95 yds) of Pingouin *Mohair/ Mohair 50* (medium weight mohair)

1 pair each of 4½ mm/No 7 and 5 mm/No 8 knitting needles

Set of four 4½ mm/No 7 double-pointed knitting needles

MEASUREMENTS

To fit 81 (86, 91, 97) cm/32 (34, 36, 38)″ bust

Length 58 (58, 59, 59) cm/22¾ (22¾, 23¼, 23¼)″

Sleeve seam 46 cm/18″

TENSION/GAUGE

17 sts and 21 rows to 10 cm/ 4″ over patt on 5 mm/No 8 needles.

BACK

With smaller needles, cast on 71 (75, 79, 83) sts and work in k1, p1 rib for 8 cm/3¼″, ending with a RS row.

Next row: (WS) [P3, k1] 1(2, 2, 3) times, p3, [k1, p twice into next st, p1, k1, p3] 8 times, [k1, p3] 2(2, 3, 3) times. 79 (83, 87, 91) sts.

Change to larger needles and cont in patt as foll:

1st row: K3, *p1, k3, rep from * to end.

2nd row: P3, *k1, p3, rep from * to end.

3rd row: K1, k2 tog, *yrn/ yo, p1, yon/yo; sl 1–k1–psso, pass the st on RH needle back on to LH needle and pass the next st over it, then return the st to RH needle – called DD, rep from * to last 4 sts, p1, yon/yo, sl 1–k1–psso, k1.

4th row: P1, *k1, p3, rep from * to last 2 sts, k1, p1.

5th row: K1, *p1, k3, rep from * to last 2 sts, p1, k1.
6th row: As 4th row.
7th row: K1, p1, *yon/yo, DD, yrn/yo, p1, rep from * to last st, k1.
8th row: As 2nd row.
Rep these 8 rows until work measures 39 cm/15¼″ from beg, ending with a WS row.

Shape armholes
Cast/bind off 6 sts at beg of next 2 rows, then 4 (4, 6, 6) sts at beg of next 2 rows.
Cont on rem 59 (63, 63, 67) sts until armholes measure 19 (19, 20, 20) cm/7½ (7½, 8, 8)″, ending with a WS row.

Shape shoulders and neck
Next row: Cast/bind off 9 sts, patt until there are 11 (12, 12, 13) sts on RH needle, turn and leave rem sts on spare needle.
Next row: Cast/bind off 4 sts, patt to end.
Cast/bind off rem 7 (8, 8, 9) sts.
Return to sts on spare needle, sl first 19 (21, 21, 23) sts on to st holder, rejoin yarn and patt to end.
Cont to match first side.

FRONT
Work as for Back until 16 rows less than Back to shoulders, ending with a WS row.

Shape neck
Next row: Patt 26 (27, 27, 28), turn and leave rem sts on spare needle.
Dec one st at neck edge on next 5 rows, then on foll 5 alt rows. 16 (17, 17, 18) sts.

Shape shoulder
Cast/bind off 9 sts at beg of next row.
Work 1 row, then cast/bind off rem 7 (8, 8, 9) sts.
Return to sts on spare needle, sl first 7 (9, 9, 11) sts on to st holder, rejoin yarn and patt to end. Cont to match first side.

SLEEVES
With smaller needles cast on 39 (39, 43, 43) sts and work in k1, p1 rib for 8 cm/3¼″, ending with an RS row.
Next row: On 3rd and 4th sizes only, p3, k1, then on all sizes, [p twice into next st, p1, k1] 12 times, p3. 51 (51, 55, 55) sts.
Change to larger needles and cont in patt as for Back, inc one st at each end of 9th and every foll 12th row, working extra sts into patt, until there are 63 (63, 67, 67) sts, then cont without shaping until sleeve measures 46 cm/18″ from beg, ending with a WS row.

Shape top/cap
Dec one st at each end of next and foll 5 (5, 6, 6) alt rows, ending with a WS row.
Cast/bind off 2 sts at beg of next 8 rows, then 4 sts at beg of next 4 rows.
Cast/bind off rem 19 (19, 21, 21) sts.

NECKBAND
Join shoulder seams.
With set of four double-pointed needles and RS facing, pick up and k33 (33, 35, 35) sts across back neck and 55 (55, 57, 57) sts around front neck, including sts on holders. Work in rounds of k1, p1 rib for 7 cm/2¾″.
Cast/bind off in rib.

ASSEMBLY
Sew in sleeves. Join side and sleeve seams.
Fold neckband in half to inside and sew in place.
Press seams lightly according to instructions on yarn band.

Soft Lace

MATERIALS
6 (6, 7, 8) 100 g/3½ oz balls (each approx 247 m/200 yds) of Twilleys *No 2 Cotton* (light weight cotton)
1 pair each of 6 mm/No 10 and 5½ mm/No 9 knitting needles
5.50 mm/size I crochet hook

MEASUREMENTS
To fit 81 (86, 91, 97) cm/32 (34, 36, 38)″ bust
Length approx 54 (54, 55, 55) cm/21¼ (21¼, 21¾, 21¾)″
Sleeve seam 46 cm/18″

TENSION/GAUGE
14 sts and 24 rows to 10 cm/4″ over patt using 6 mm/No 10 needles.

ABBREVIATIONS
K1b = knit 1 below by knitting into centre of st on row below next stitch.

BACK
With smaller needles, cast on 50 (54, 58, 62) sts and work for 8 cm/3¼″ in k2, p2 rib, ending with a WS row.
Next row: Rib, inc 16 sts evenly across row. 66 (70, 74, 78) sts.
Change to larger needles and beg patt as foll:
1st row: (WS) K.
2nd row: K1, *k1b, k1, rep from * to last st, k1.
3rd row: K.
4th row: K2, *k1b, k1, rep from * to end.
These 4 rows form patt. Cont in patt without shaping until work measures 35 cm/13¾″ from beg, ending with an RS row.

Shape armholes
Keeping patt correct, dec one st at each end of next and every other row until 22 (26, 26, 30) sts rem.
Patt 1 row, p next row.
Leave rem sts on spare needle.

FRONT
Work as for Back.

SLEEVES
With smaller needles, cast on 30 (30, 34, 34) sts and work 8 cm/3¼″ in k2, p2 rib, ending with a WS row.
Next row: Rib, inc 32 sts evenly across row. 62 (62, 66, 66) sts.
Change to larger needles and work in patt as for Back and Front until work measures 46 cm/18″ from beg, ending with a RS row.

Shape top/cap
Keeping patt correct, dec one st at each end of next and every other row until 18 sts rem.
Patt 1 row, p next row.
Leave rem sts on spare needle.

NECKBAND
With RS of work facing and smaller needles, k sts from one sleeve, then across front, 2nd sleeve and back. 80 (88, 88, 96) sts.
Work 3 rows in k2, p2 rib.
Next row: *K2 tog, yrn/yo, p2, rep from * to end. Work 2 rows more in rib.
Cast/bind off in rib.

TIE
With crochet hook and 2 strands of yarn, make a chain about 140 cm/55″ long.
Fasten off.

ASSEMBLY
Do not press.
Join shoulder, side and sleeve seams.
Sew in sleeves.
Press seams lightly.
Thread cord through neck holes and tie.

Frilled Top

MATERIALS
8 (8, 9, 9) 50 g/1¾ oz balls (each approx 50 m/108 yds) of Robin *Thermospun* (chunky/bulky weight yarn)
1 pair each of 4½ mm/No 7 and 6 mm/No 10 knitting needles
6 mm/No 10 circular knitting needle
6 buttons
Beads or crystals for decoration as required

MEASUREMENTS
To fit 81 (86, 91, 97) cm/32 (34, 36, 38)″ bust
Length 64 cm/25¼″

TENSION/GAUGE
14 sts and 22 rows to 10 cm/4″ over patt using 6 mm/No 10 needles.

BACK
With smaller needles, cast on 54 (58, 62, 66) sts.

1st row: K2, *p2, k2, rep from * to end.

2nd row: P2, *k2, p2, rep from * to end.

Rep these 2 rows for 13 cm/5", ending with a WS row and inc one st in last row. 55 (59, 63, 67) sts.

Change to larger needles.

Next row: K1 (3, 5, 7), [inc in next st, k3] 13 times, inc in next st, k1 (3, 5, 7). 69 (73, 77, 81) sts.

Next row: P.

Cont in patt as foll:

1st row: K2, *p1, k3, rep from * to last 3 sts, p1, k2.

Beg with a p row, work 3 rows in st st.

5th row: P1, *k3, p1, rep from * to end.

Work 3 rows in st st.

Rep these 8 rows 5 times more.

Shape sleeve

Keeping patt correct throughout, inc one st at each end of next and foll 3 alt rows, ending with a p row, then cast on 8 sts at beg of next 2 rows. 93 (97, 101, 105) sts.

Cont in patt until work measures 59 cm/23¼" from beg, ending with a p row.

Shape shoulder

Keeping patt correct, dec one st at each end of next and every other row until 83 (97, 91, 95) sts rem, ending with a p row.

Cast/bind off loosely.

FRONT

Work as for Back.

RUFFLE (make 2)

With circular needle cast on 264 (270, 276, 282) sts and work 4 rows in g st, then cont in st st until work measures 2.5 cm/1" from beg, ending with a p row.

Next row: K2 tog to end.

Cast/bind off.

ASSEMBLY

Do not press.

Join side and underarm seams. Join the two pieces of ruffle and sew to top edge of sweater as in picture.

Leaving approx 30 cm/11¾" open in centre for neck, join shoulders as far as end of shaping, then sew 3 buttons to each shoulder.

Sew on beads and/or crystals as required.

Cassata Waistcoat

MATERIALS

3 (3, 3, 4, 4, 4) 100 g/3½ oz balls (each approx 160 m/ 175 yds) of Twilleys *D42 Cotton* (medium weight cotton) in main colour (M)

2 50 g/1¾ oz balls (each approx 128 m/140 yds) of Twilleys *Stalite* (light weight cotton) in 1st contrast colour (A)

1 (1, 2, 2, 2, 2) balls of *Stalite* in 2nd contrast colour (B)

1 (1, 1, 2, 2, 2) balls of *Stalite* in 3rd contrast colour (C)

3 mm/No 2 and 3¼ mm/No 3 circular knitting needles

6 buttons

MEASUREMENTS

To fit 81 (86, 91, 97, 102, 107) cm/32 (34, 36, 38, 40, 42)" bust or chest

Length 65 (65, 68, 68, 71, 71) cm/25½ (25½, 26¾, 26¾, 28, 28)"

TENSION/GAUGE

22 sts and 32 rows to 10 cm/4" over stripe patt using 3¼ mm/No 3 needles.

Note: Back and Fronts are worked back and forth in rows on circular needle in one piece to armholes.

MAIN BODY

With smaller circular needle and M, cast on 165 (173, 183, 191, 201, 209) sts.

1st row: K1, *p1, k1, rep from * to end.

2nd row: P1, *k1, p1, rep from * to end.

Rep these 2 rows for 6 cm/2½", ending with a 1st row.

Next row: Rib 1 (1, 3, 3, 5, 5), * work twice into next st, rib

3, rep from * to end. 206 (216, 228, 238, 250, 260) sts.

Change to larger circular needle and cont in stripe patt as foll:

(**Note:** Join in a 2nd ball of M at opposite end and carry a ball of M up each side of work, but break off contrast colours after each stripe.)

1st–3rd rows: With B, beg with a k row, work 3 rows st st.

4th–7th rows: With M, beg with a p row, work 4 rows st st.

8th–10th rows: With A, work 3 rows g st.

11th row: With M, k 1 row.

12th and 13th rows: With C and beg with a p row, work 2 rows st st.

14th–16th rows: With M, work 3 rows g st.

17th row: With B, k 1 row.

18th and 19th rows: With M and beg with a p row, work 2 rows st st.

20th–22nd rows: With A, work 3 rows g st.

23rd row: With M, k 1 row.

24th and 25th rows: With C and beg with a p row, work 2 rows st st.

26th–28th rows: With M and beg with a p row, work 3 rows st st.

29th–31st rows: With B, work 3 rows g st.

32nd and 33rd rows: With M, work 2 rows g st.

34th–36th rows: With A and beg with a p row, work 3 rows st st.

37th and 38th rows: With M, work 2 rows g st.

39th and 40th rows: With C and beg with a k row, work 2 rows st st.

41st–44th rows: With M, work 4 rows g st.

These 44 rows form stripe patt and are rep throughout.

Cont in patt until work measures 33 (33, 35, 35, 37, 37) cm/13 (13, 13¾, 13¾, 14½, 14½)" from beg, ending with a WS row.

Shape front edge

Next row: K1, sl 1–k1–psso, patt to last 3 sts, k2 tog, k1.

Work 3 rows.

Rep last 4 rows 3 times more. 198 (208, 220, 230, 242, 252) sts.

Divide for armholes

Next row: K1, sl 1–k1–psso, patt 43 (45, 48, 51, 54, 56), cast/bind off 4 sts, patt 98 (104, 110, 114, 120, 126) including st on needle after casting/binding off, cast/bind off 4 sts, patt to last 3 sts, k2 tog, k1.

Cont on last 45 (47, 50, 53, 56, 58) sts for Left Front, dec one st at armhole edge on next 4 rows, and cont to dec at front edge as before on every 4th row until 27 (30, 32, 34, 36, 39) sts rem.

Cont without shaping until armhole measures 27 (27, 28, 28, 29, 29) cm/10¾ (10¾, 11, 11, 11½, 11½)″, ending with a WS row.
Cast/bind off.

Return to 98 (104, 110, 114, 120, 126) sts for Back and with WS facing, rejoin yarn and patt to end.

Dec one st at each end of next 4 rows. 90 (96, 102, 106, 112, 118) sts.

Cont without shaping until armhole measures same as for Front, ending with a WS row.

Shape shoulders
Cast/bind off 27 (30, 32, 34, 36, 39) sts at beg of next 2 rows.
Cast/bind off rem 36 (36, 38, 38, 40, 40) sts.
Return to rem sts for Right Front and work to match Left Front, reversing shaping.

FRONT BORDER
Join shoulder seams.
Mark position of buttons on front edge – the first on 5th row from beg, the 2nd approx 2 cm/¾″ below beg of front shaping, then 4 more at equal intervals between these 2.
With smaller needle and M, cast on 7 sts and work 4 rows in rib as for Main Body.
5th row: Rib 2, cast/bind off 2 sts, rib 3.
6th row: Rib 3, cast on 2 sts, rib 2.
Cont in rib, make 5 more buttonholes to correspond with positions marked, then cont until border, when slightly stretched, reaches up front edge, around back neck and down other front. Cast/bind off in rib.

ARMHOLE BORDERS
With smaller needles and M, cast on 107 (107, 111, 111, 117, 117) sts and work 6 rows in rib as for Main Body. Cast/bind off in rib.

ASSEMBLY
Press pieces with a warm iron over a damp cloth, omitting ribbing.
Sew on front border, placing button-holes on Right Front for woman's version or on Left Front for man's version.
Sew on armhole borders, joining sides of borders at centre of cast/bound-off sts at armholes.
Press seams. Sew on buttons.

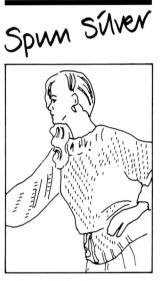

Spun Silver

MATERIALS
14 (15, 16) 50 g/1¾ oz balls (each approx 100 m/109 yds) of Twilleys *Double Gold* (medium weight metallic yarn)
1 pair each of 4½ mm/No 7 and 4 mm/No 6 knitting needles
4.00 mm/size F crochet hook
Elastic for cuffs
Lace for collar

MEASUREMENTS
To fit 81 (86, 91) cm/32 (34, 36)″ bust
Length approx 68 cm/26¾″
Sleeve seam approx 43 cm/17″

TENSION/GAUGE
22 sts and 32 rows to 10 cm/4″ over patt using 4½ mm/No 7 needles.

BACK
With smaller needles, cast on 96 (104, 112) sts and work 4 cm/1½″ in k2, p2 rib.
Change to larger needles and beg patt as foll:
1st–4th rows: *K4, p4, rep from * to end.
5th row: P2, *k4, p4, rep from * to last 6 sts, k4, p2.
6th row: K2, *p4, k4, rep from * to last 6 sts, p4, k2.
Rep last 2 rows once more.
9th–12th rows: *P4, k4, rep from * to end.
13th row: As 6th row.
14th row: As 5th row.
Rep last 2 rows once more.
These 16 rows form patt.
Cont without shaping until work measures approx 23 cm/9″ from beg, ending with a 12th patt row.
Change to smaller needles and work 4 rows in k2, p2 rib.
Next row: *K2, yrn/yo, p2 tog, rep from * to end. Work 3 more rows in rib.
Change back to larger needles and beg with a 13th patt row, cont in patt until work measures 68 cm/26¾″, ending with a WS row.
Cast/bind off loosely.

FRONT
Work as for Back until Front is 8 rows less than Back, ending with WS row.

Shape neck
Next row: Patt 28 (32, 36), cast/bind off next 40 sts, patt 28 (32, 36) sts.
Work on last set of sts, dec one st at neck edge on next 7 rows.
Cast/bind off loosely.
Rejoin yarn to other sts and work to match first side.

SLEEVES
Using larger needles, cast on 96 sts and work in patt as for Back, beg with 1st row, for 43 cm/17″, ending with a WS row.
Cast/bind off loosely.

ASSEMBLY
Press work.
Join shoulder seams.
Sew cast/bound-off edge of sleeves to sides of Back and Front beg and ending 22 cm/8¾″ each side of shoulder seam.
Join side and sleeve seams. Press seams.
Using crochet hook, work 3 rounds of firm dc/sc around neck edge. Fasten off.
For belt, with crochet hook, work in ch for 142 cm/56″ and then work 1 row of dc/sc into ch, then 1 row of dc/sc on dc/sc. Fasten off.
Thread tie through holes at waist and tie at front.
Gather bottom of sleeves with elastic to fit wrist or omit elastic and turn back

10 cm/4″ cuff.
Sew lace to neck edge.

A Bigger Splash

MATERIALS
5 (6, 6) 100 g/3½ oz balls (each approx 155 m/170 yds) of Twilleys *Pegasus 8-ply cotton* (medium weight cotton)
1 pair each of 3¼ mm/No 3 and 7 mm/No 10½ knitting needles
3.50 mm/size E crochet hook
4 buttons

MEASUREMENTS
To fit 81 (86, 91) cm/32 (34, 36)″ bust
Length 61 (63, 65) cm/24 (24¾, 25½)″
Sleeve seam 46 cm/18″

TENSION/GAUGE
16 sts and 18 rows to 10 cm/4″ over rib using 7 mm/No 10½ needles, measured with rib slightly stretched.

BACK
With smaller needles, cast on 77 (81, 85) sts.
1st row: (RS) K1, *p1, k1, rep from * to end.
2nd row: P1, *k1, p1, rep from * to end.
Rep these 2 rows 7 times more.
Change to larger needles and cont in rib until work measures 38 cm/15″ from beg, ending with a 2nd row.

Shape armholes
Cast/bind off 2 sts at beg of next 2 rows.
Next row: K1, p1, sl 1–k1–psso, rib to last 4 sts, k2 tog, p1, k1.
Next row: P1, k1, p1, rib to last 3 sts, p1, k1, p1.
Rep these 2 rows until 33 sts

67

rem, ending with a WS row.
Leave sts on st holder.

FRONT
Work as for Back until 41 sts rem, ending with a RS row.

Shape neck
Next row: Rib 10, turn and leave rem sts on spare needle.
Next row: K2 tog, rib 4, k2 tog, p1, k1.
Next row: P1, k1, p1, rib 3, p2 tog.
Next row: K2 tog, p1, k2 tog, p1, k1.
Next row: P1, k1, p1, p2 tog.
Dec one st at neck edge on next 2 rows, then k2 tog and fasten off.
Return to sts on spare needle, sl centre 21 sts on to st holder, rejoin yarn and patt to end. Cont to match first side.

SLEEVES
With smaller needles cast on 43 (45, 47) sts and work 8 rows in rib as for Back.
Change to larger needles and cont in rib, inc one st at each end of next and every foll 6th row until there are 55 (59, 63) sts, then cont without shaping until sleeve measures 46 cm/18″ from beg, ending with a WS row.

Shape top/cap
Cast/bind off 2 sts at beg of next 2 rows, then dec as for Back at each end of next and every other row until 11 sts rem, ending with a WS row.
Leave sts on st holder.

NECKBAND
Join raglan seams, leaving Left Front raglan open.
With smaller needles and RS facing, pick up and k11 sts down Left Front neck, k front neck sts, pick up and k10 sts up Right Front neck, then k sts of right sleeve, back neck and left sleeve, knitting 2 tog at each back raglan seam. 95 sts.
Beg next row with p1, work 5 rows in k1, p1 rib.
Cast/bind off in rib.

ASSEMBLY
Join Left Front raglan seam for about 3 (5, 7) cm/1¼ (2, 2¾)″.
With crochet hook, work 20 dc/sc down sleeve edge of opening, then 20 dc/sc up front edge, turn.
Next row: Work 2 dc/sc, [3 ch, miss/skip 1 dc/sc, 4 dc/sc] 3 times, 3 ch, miss/skip 1 dc/sc, 2 dc/sc. Fasten off.
Join side and sleeve seams.
Do not press.
Sew on buttons.

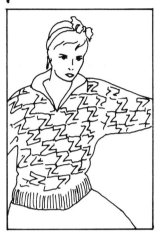

MATERIALS
Skirt:
8 (9) 50 g/1¾ oz balls (each approx 105 m/115 yds) of Lister–Lee *Motoravia DK* (double knitting/knitting worsted weight yarn)
3 mm/No 2, 3¼ mm/No 3 and 4 mm/No 6 circular knitting needles
Waist length of elastic

Sweater:
10 (11) 40 g/1½ oz balls (each approx 71 m/78 yds) of Lister–Lee *Poodle* (medium weight bouclé) in main colour (M)
4 (5) balls in contrast colour (C)
1 50 g/1¾ oz ball of Lister–Lee *Motoravia DK* (double knitting/knitting worsted weight yarn) in colour to match main colour (A)
1 pair each of 3¼ mm/No 3 and 5 mm/No 8 knitting needles
5 mm/No 8 circular knitting needle

MEASUREMENTS
To fit 81–86 (91–97) cm/32–34 (36–38)″ bust
Skirt length 56 cm/22″
Sweater length 61 cm/24″
Sleeve seam 45 cm/17¾″

TENSION/GAUGE
Skirt:
22 sts and 28 rows to 10 cm/4″ over st st using 4 mm/No 6 needles.

Pullover:
16 sts and 24 rows to 10 cm/4″ over st st using 5 mm/No 8 needles and M.
16 sts and approx 18 rows to 10 cm/4″ over patt using 5 mm/No 8 needles and M.

SKIRT
Instructions:
With 4 mm/No 6 circular needle, cast on 312 (336) sts and join into a round.
Work in rounds of k2, p2 rib for 3 cm/1¼″, ending at end of a round.
Cont in rounds of st st (k every round) until work measures 41 cm/16¼″ from beg, adjusting length here if required.
Place marker at end of last round.
Next round: *K1, k2 tog, rep from * to end. 208 (224) sts.
Cont in rounds of k2, p2 rib until work measures 5 cm/2″ from marker.
Change to 3¼ mm/No 3 circular needle and cont in rib until work measures 10 cm/4″ from marker.
Change to 3 mm/No 2 circular needle and cont in rib until work measures 15 cm/6″ from marker.
Cast/bind off in rib.

ASSEMBLY
Omitting ribbing, press work according to instructions on yarn band.
Sew elastic inside waist with a herringbone st casing.

SWEATER

BACK
With smaller needles and A, cast on 90 (98) sts.
1st row: K2, *p2, k2, rep from * to end.
2nd row: P2, *k2, p2, rep from * to end.
Rep these 2 rows for 7 cm/2¾″, ending with a 1st row.
Next row: P2 (6), *p2 tog, p2, rep from * to last 0 (4) sts, p0 (4). 68 (76) sts. Break off A, join in M and C, change to larger needles and beg with a k row, cont in st st, working in patt from chart until work measures 32 cm/12½″ from beg, ending with a p row.

Shape sleeves
Keeping patt correct, inc one st at each end of next 6 rows. 80 (88) sts.
Change to circular needle

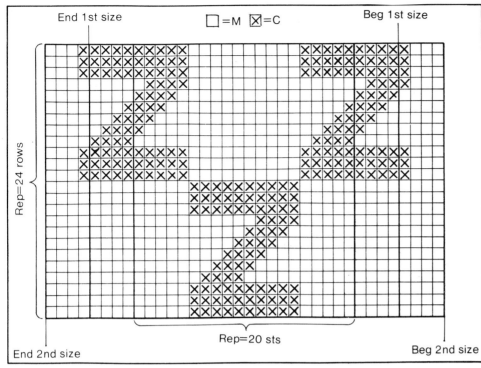

Repeat motif used on Motorbiking sweater, back and front.

and cast on 13 sts at beg of next 8 rows. 184 (192) sts.** Work 36 rows in patt.

Shape upper sleeve and shoulders

Cast/bind off 8 sts at beg of next 12 rows, then 8 (9) sts at beg of foll 8 rows.
Cont on rem 24 sts for 5 cm/ 2″, ending with a RS row.
K 1 row to mark turning line. Break off C. Beg with a k row, cont in st st in M for 5 cm/2″.
Cast/bind off.

FRONT

Work as for Back to **, then work 26 rows in patt.

Divide for neck

Next row: K92 (96), turn and leave rem sts on spare needle.
Cont on these sts, work 9 rows.

Shape upper sleeve and shoulder

Cast/bind off 8 sts at beg of next and foll 5 alt rows, then 8 (9) sts at beg of foll 4 alt rows.
Cont on rem 12 sts for 5 cm/ 2″, ending with an RS row.
K 1 row to mark turning line. Break off C. Beg with a k row, cont in st st in M for 18 cm/7″ for front facing.
Cast/bind off.
Return to sts on spare needle

and work to match, reversing all shaping.

CUFFS

Join upper sleeve and shoulder seams.
With $3\frac{1}{4}$ mm/No 3 needles, A and RS facing, pick up and k58 sts evenly along edge of sleeve.
Beg with a 2nd row, work in rib as for Back for 7 cm/2¾″.
Cast/bind off in rib.

ASSEMBLY

Do not press.
Join side and underarm seams.
Join edges of collar, fold to inside on turning line and stitch facings in place.

MATERIALS

3 50 g/1¾ oz balls (each approx 115 m/126 yds) of Jaeger Cotton Flammé (DK weight cotton) in main colour (M)

4 25 g/1 oz balls (each approx 112 m/123 yds) of Twilleys Lyscordet (light weight cotton) in 1st contrast colour (A)

3 25 g/1 oz balls (approx 51 m/ 56 yds) of Jaeger Mohair Spun (light weight mohair) in 2nd contrast colour (B)

1 pair each of $3\frac{1}{4}$ mm/No 3 and $4\frac{1}{2}$ mm/No 7 knitting needles

MEASUREMENTS

To fit 81–91 cm/32–36″ bust
Length 44 cm/17¼″

TENSION/GAUGE

16 sts and 19 rows to 10 cm/ 4″ over patt using $4\frac{1}{2}$ mm/ No 7 needles.

BACK

With smaller needles and A, cast on 84 sts. Work 8 cm/3¼″ in k1, p1 rib. Change to larger needles and B.
1st row: Inc in first st, k10, [k1, p1, k1] all into next st, turn, k3, turn, p3, turn, k3 tog = one bobble made, called MB, *k11, MB, rep from * to last 11 sts, k10, inc in last st.

2nd row: Using A, p to end.
3rd row: K to end, inc one st at each end.
4th–10th rows: Using M and beg with a p row, work 7 rows in st st, inc one st at both ends of every k row.
These 10 rows form patt.
Rep these 10 rows twice more, inc as before and working bobbles on 1st patt row so that they are directly above each other, working extra sts in st st. 114 sts.
Cont in patt without shaping for 24 rows, so ending with a 4th patt row.

Shape shoulders

Keeping patt correct, cast/ bind off 5 sts at beg of next 10 rows. 64 sts.

Shape neck

Cast/bind off 5 sts, k8, k2 tog, k1, turn, leaving rem sts on spare needle.
Next row: P1, p2 tog, p to end.
Next row: Cast/bind off 5 sts, k to last 3 sts, k2 tog, k1.
Next row: P1, p2 tog.
Next row: Cast/bind off.
With RS of work facing, sl centre 32 sts on to a st holder until required for neckband. Rejoin yarn to rem 16 sts and complete to match first side, reversing shaping.

FRONT

Work as for Back.

NECKBAND

Join right shoulder seam. With RS facing, smaller needles and A, pick up and k6 sts down Left Front neck edge, k across 32 sts on st holder, pick up and k6 sts up Right Front edge, 6 sts down Right Back neck edge, k across 32 sts on other st holder and pick up and k6 sts up Left Back neck edge. 88 sts.
Work 5 rows in k1, p1, rib.
Cast/bind off loosely in rib.

ARMBANDS

Join left shoulder seam and neckband.
Using smaller needles and A, pick up and k50 sts along row edges of sleeves (straight edge).
Work 5 rows in k1, p1, rib.
Cast/bind off loosely in rib.

ASSEMBLY

Do not press.
Join side and sleeve seams.

MATERIALS

8 (9) 25 g/1 oz balls (each approx 53 m/58 yds) of Argyll *Finesse Mohair* (medium weight mohair) in main colour (A)

4 balls in each of 2 contrast colours (B and C)

1 pair each of 4½ mm/No 7 and 5½ mm/No 9 knitting needles

REMINDER

In all the patterns in this book the British terminology, where it differs from American usage, is given first and the corresponding American term follows. An oblique line separates the two. For example: cast/bind off.

Measurements in both metric and in inches and yards are given throughout, also separated by an oblique line. For example: 2.5 cm/1″.

Readers are asked to pay particular attention to information in the Introduction regarding pattern abbreviations, yarn descriptions and yarn substitution.

MEASUREMENTS

To fit 81–86 (91–97) cm/32–34 (36–38)″ bust

Length 56 (60) cm/22¼ (24)″

Sleeve seam 44 cm/17¾″

TENSION/GAUGE

16 sts and 22 rows to 10 cm/4″ over st st using 5½ mm/No 9 needles.

Note: When working from chart, use separate balls for each section and twist colours where they join on every row to prevent holes.

BACK

With smaller needles and B, cast on 67 (75) sts.

1st row: (RS) K1, *p1, k1, rep from * to end.

2nd row: P1, *k1, p1, rep from * to end.

Rep these 2 rows for 10 cm/4″, ending with a 1st row.

Next row: Rib 6, *inc 1 by picking up loop between sts and working into the back of it, rib 6 (7), rep from * 8 times more, inc 1, rib to end. 77 (85) sts.

Break off B.

Change to larger needles, join in A and beg with a k row, work 32 rows in st st.

33rd row: K38 (42) A, 1B, 38 (42) A.

Cont working in patt from chart (beg with 34th row) as far as row 50.

Shape armholes

Cont in B, cast/bind off 3 sts at beg of next 2 rows.

Dec one st at each end of next and every 4th row until 65 (71) sts rem, then at each end of every other row until 27 (29) sts rem, ending with a p row.

Leave sts on st holder.

FRONT

Using C instead of B, work as for Back until 45 (47) sts rem, ending with a p row.

Shape neck

Next row: K2 tog, k16 (17), turn and leave rem sts on spare needle.

Next row: P2 tog, p to end.

Cont to dec at neck edge on next 3 rows, then on every other row, and AT THE SAME TIME dec at armhole edge as before on every other row until 5 (4) sts rem. Keeping neck edge straight cont to dec at armhole edge on every other row until 2 sts

rem, ending with a p row.

Cast/bind off.

Return to sts on spare needle, sl centre 9 sts on to st holder, rejoin yarn and k to last 2 sts, k2 tog.

Cont to match first side.

LEFT SLEEVE

With smaller needles and A, cast on 31 (33) sts and work in rib as for Back for 6 cm/2½″, ending with a 1st row.

Next row: Rib 2, [inc 1, rib 1] 3 times, [inc 1, rib 2] 11 times, [inc 1, rib 1] 3 times, rib 1 (3). 48 (50) sts.

Change to larger needles and beg with a k row cont in st st, work 8 rows A, 4 rows C, 4 rows A, 4 rows C, 46 rows A, and AT THE SAME TIME inc one st at each end of every 14th row.

67th row: K27 (28) A, 1B, 1C, 27 (28) A.

Cont in patt from chart, inc at each end of 70th row. 58 (60) sts.

Then cont in patt to row 84.

Shape top/cap

Cont in B and C as on chart, cast/bind off 3 sts at beg of next 2 rows.

Dec at each end of next and every 4th row until 46 (42) sts rem, then at each end of every other row until 8 sts rem, ending with a p row.

Leave sts on st holder.

RIGHT SLEEVE

Work to match left sleeve, using B instead of C for stripes, and reversing B and C at top.

NECKBAND

Join raglan seams, leaving left back raglan seam open.

With smaller needles and A, k sts of left sleeve, pick up and k14 sts down Left Front neck, k front neck sts, pick up and k14 sts up Right Front neck, then k sts of right sleeve and back neck, knitting 2 tog at seam. 79 (81) sts.

K 1 row.

Work in rib as for Back for 9 cm/3½″.

Cast/bind off loosely in rib.

ASSEMBLY

Join left back raglan seam and neckband. Join side and sleeve seams.

Fold neckband in half to inside and sew in place.

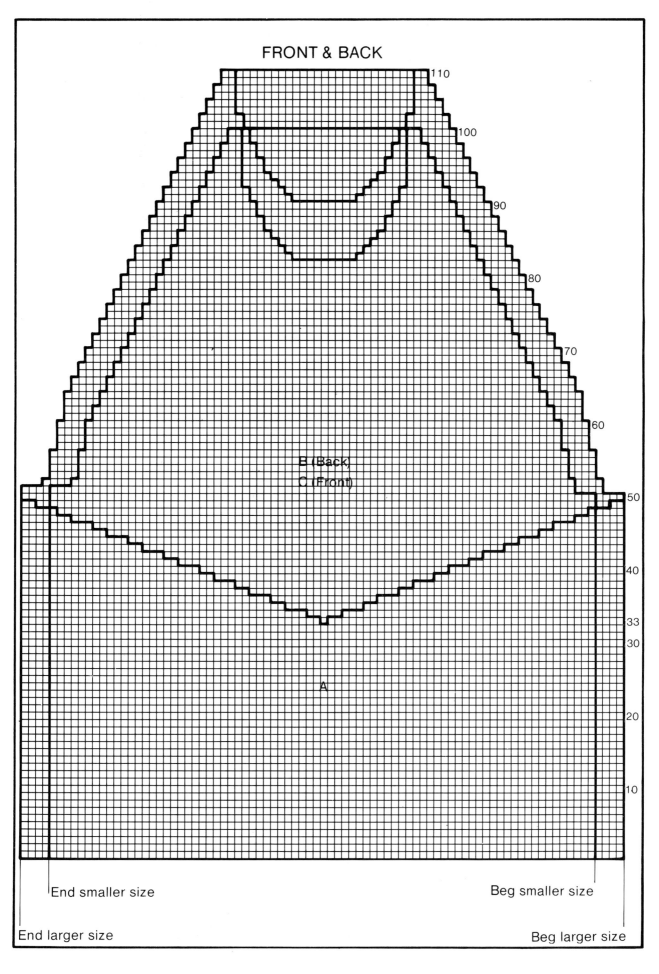

FRONT & BACK

110

100

90

80

70

60

B (Back)
C (Front)

50

40

33
30

A

20

10

End smaller size   Beg smaller size

End larger size   Beg larger size

SLEEVE

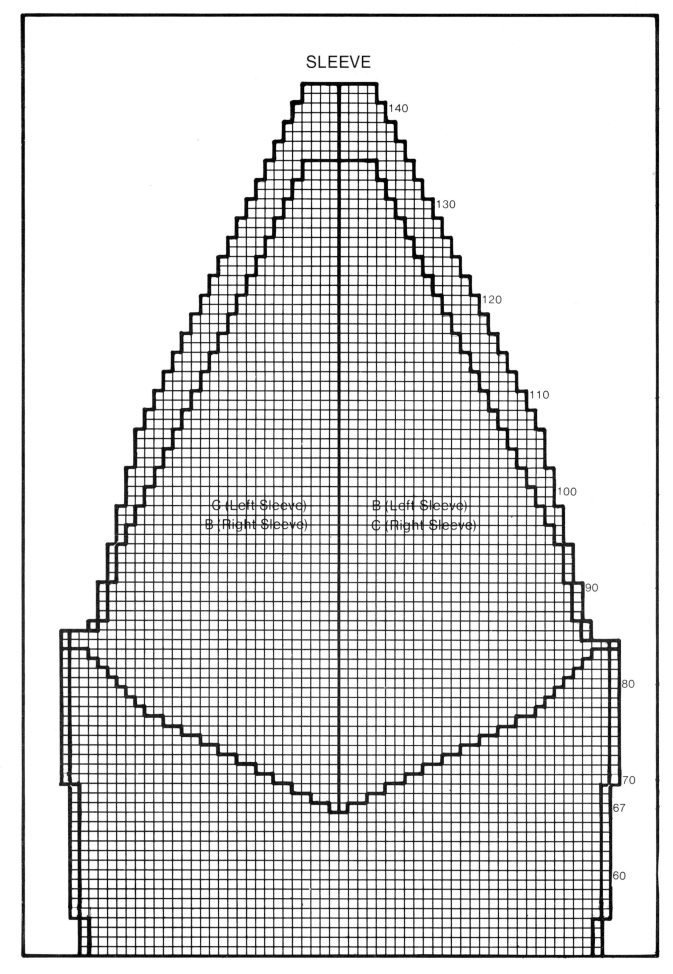

C (Left Sleeve)   B (Left Sleeve)
B (Right Sleeve) C (Right Sleeve)

140
130
120
110
100
90
80
70
67
60

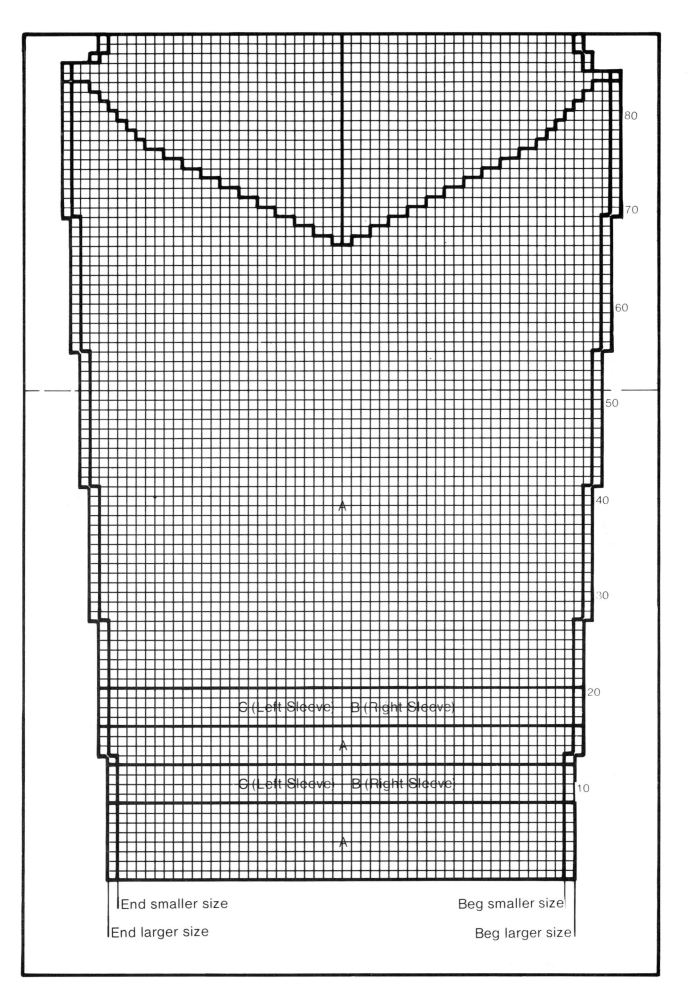

80

70

60

50

40

30

20

C (Left Sleeve)   B (Right Sleeve)

A

10

C (Left Sleeve)   B (Right Sleeve)

A

A

End smaller size   Beg smaller size

End larger size   Beg larger size

Bargello

MATERIALS
4 (5, 6) 25 g/1 oz balls (each approx 53.25 m/58.5 yds) of Argyll *Finesse* (medium weight mohair) in main colour (M)

2 (2, 3) balls in 1st contrast colour (A)

3 (3, 4) balls in 2nd contrast colour (B)

3 balls each in 3rd, 4th and 5th contrast colours (C, D and E)

3 (4, 5) balls in 6th contrast colour (F)

2 (2, 3) balls in 7th contrast colour (G)

1 pair each of $4\frac{1}{2}$ mm/No 7 and 6 mm/No 10 knitting needles

Set of four $4\frac{1}{2}$ mm/No 7 double-pointed knitting needles

MEASUREMENTS
To fit 81 (86, 91) cm/32 (34, 36)" bust

Length 59 (60, 61) cm/$23\frac{1}{4}$ ($23\frac{3}{4}$, 24)"

Sleeve seam 49 cm/$19\frac{1}{4}$"

TENSION/GAUGE
17 sts and 22 rows to 10 cm/4" over patt using 6 mm/No 10 needles.

BACK
With smaller needles and M, cast on 67 (69, 71) sts.

1st row: K1, *p1, k1, rep from * to end.

2nd row: P1, *k1, p1, rep from * to end.

Rep these 2 rows for 5 cm/2", ending with a 1st row.

Next row: [Rib 1, inc 1 by picking up loop between sts and k into the back of it] 5 (8, 11) times, [rib 2, inc 1] 28 (26, 24) times, [rib 1, inc 1] 5 (8,

11) times, p1. 105 (111, 117) sts.

Change to larger needles and beg with a k row, cont in st st, working in patt from chart until work measures 38 cm/15" from beg, ending with a p row.

(**Note:** Beg working chart from chart row 1, reading odd numbered rows from right to left and even rows from left to right. After working 60 rows of chart, rep again from row 18.)

Shape armholes
Keeping patt correct, cast/bind off 7 sts at beg of next 2 rows. 91 (97, 103) sts.**

Cont without shaping until armholes measure 21 (22, 23) cm/$8\frac{1}{4}$ ($8\frac{3}{4}$, 9)", ending with a p row.

Shape shoulders
Cast/bind off 27 (29, 31) sts at beg of next 2 rows.

Leave rem 37 (39, 41) sts on holder.

FRONT
Work as for Back as far as **.

Divide for neck
Next row: K45 (48, 51), turn and leave rem sts on spare needle.

Dec one st at neck edge on next 13 (15, 17) rows, then on every other row until 27 (29, 31) sts rem. Cont without shaping until armhole measures as for Back, ending with a p row.

Cast/bind off.

Return to sts on spare needle, sl first st (Centre Front) on to st holder, rejoin yarn and k to end in patt.

Cont to match first side.

SLEEVES
With smaller needles and M, cast on 33 (33, 37) sts and work in rib as for Back for 5 cm/2", ending with a 1st row.

Next row: [Rib 1, inc 1] twice, [rib 2, inc 1] 14 (14, 16) times, [rib 1, inc 1] twice, p1. 51 (51, 57) sts.

Change to larger needles and beg with a k row, cont in patt from chart for 2nd (2nd, 3rd) size of Back, and inc one st at each end of every 3rd row until there are 93 (97, 101) sts, then cont without shaping until sleeve measures 52 cm/

$20\frac{1}{2}$" from beg, ending with a p row.

Cast/bind off loosely.

NECKBAND
Join shoulder seams. With set of four double-pointed needles and M, RS facing, k back neck sts, dec 8 sts evenly across them, pick up and k45 (47, 49) sts down Left Front neck, k Centre Front st from st holder, then pick up and k45 (47, 49) sts up Right Front neck. 120 (126, 132) sts.

Next round: Work in k1, p1 rib to 2 sts before Centre Front, p2 tog, k1, p2 tog tb1, rib to end.

Rep this round for 3 cm/$1\frac{1}{4}$", then cast/bind off in rib, still dec at Centre Front.

ASSEMBLY
Sew in sleeves.

Join side and sleeve seams, sewing 3 cm/$1\frac{1}{4}$" of sleeve seams to the cast off stitches at armholes.

Subtle Texture

MATERIALS
8 (9, 10) 25 g/1 oz balls (each approx 59 m/65 yds) of Jaeger *Mohair Spun* (medium weight mohair) in 1st colour (A)

2 balls in 2nd colour (B)

3 (3, 4) balls in 3rd colour (C)

2 (2, 3) 50 g/$1\frac{3}{4}$ oz balls (each approx 120 m/131 yds) of Jaeger *Luxury Spun DK* (double knitting/knitting worsted weight) in both 4th and 5th colours (D and E)

1 pair each of $3\frac{1}{4}$ mm/No 3, 4 mm/No 6, $4\frac{1}{2}$ mm/No 7 and $5\frac{1}{2}$ mm/No 9 knitting needles

MEASUREMENTS
To fit 81–86 (86–91, 91–97)

cm/32–34 (34–36, 36–38)″
bust
Length 63 (64, 65) cm/24$\frac{3}{4}$
(25$\frac{1}{4}$, 25$\frac{3}{4}$)″
Sleeve seam 43 cm/17″

TENSION/GAUGE
22 sts and 30 rows to 10 cm/
4″ over st st using 4 mm/No 6
needles and D.
16 sts and 21 rows to 10 cm/4″
over st st using 5$\frac{1}{2}$ mm/No 9
needles and A.

ABBREVIATIONS
MB = make bobble – k into
front, back, front and back
of next st making 4 sts, turn,
k4, turn, p4, turn, [k2 tog]
twice, turn, p2 tog.

BACK
With 4$\frac{1}{2}$ mm/No 7 needles
and A, cast on 74 (78, 82) sts.
1st row: K2, *p2, k2, rep
from * to end.
2nd row: P2, *k2, p2, rep
from * to end.
Rep these 2 rows 5 times
more, then 1st row again.
Next row: Rib 9, [inc in next
st, rib 1] 28 (30, 32) times, inc
in next st, rib 8. 103 (109, 115)
sts.
Change to 3$\frac{1}{4}$ mm/No 3
needles and D and work 4
rows in g st.
Change to 4 mm/No 6 needles
and E and beg with a k row,
work 4 rows in st st.
9th row: K1C, *5B, 1C, rep
from * to end.
10th row: P2C, *3B, 3C, rep
from * to last 5 sts, 3B, 2C.
11th row: K1B, *2C, 1B, rep
from * to end.
12th row: P2B, *3C, 3B, rep
from * to last 5 sts, 3C, 2B.
13th row: K3B, *1C, 5B, rep
from * to last 4 sts, 1C, 3B.
Using E, beg with a p row
and work 5 rows in st st.
Change to 3$\frac{1}{4}$ mm/No 3
needles and D and work 4
rows in g st.
Change to 4 mm/No 6 needles
and beg with a k row, work
in st st as foll:
23rd row: K3A, *1E, 5A, rep
from * to last 4 sts, 1E, 3A.
24th row: P2A, *3E, 3A, rep
from * to last 5 sts, 3E, 2A.
25th row: K1A, *5E, 1A, rep
from * to end.
26th row: P in E.
27th row: K3E, *MB in A,
k5E, rep from * to last 4 sts,
MB in A, k3E.
28th row: P as 25th.
29th row: K as 24th.
30th row: P as 23rd.

Change to 3$\frac{1}{4}$ mm/No 3
needles and D and work 4
rows in g st.
Change to 4 mm/No 6 needles
and rep 23rd–30th rows, but
using C instead of A and D
instead of E.
These 42 rows form patt and
are rep throughout.
Cont in patt until work measures 43 cm/17″ from beg,
ending with a WS row.

Shape armholes
Keeping patt correct, cast/
bind off 5 (6, 7) sts at beg of
next 2 rows.
Dec one st at each end of
next 3 rows, then foll 3 alt
rows. 81 (85, 89) sts.
Cont without shaping until
armholes measure 20 (21, 22)
cm/7$\frac{3}{4}$ (8$\frac{1}{4}$, 8$\frac{3}{4}$)″, ending with a
WS row.

Shape shoulders
Cast/bind off 9 sts at beg of
next 4 rows, then 8 (9, 10) sts
at beg of next 2 rows.
Leave rem 29 (31, 33) sts on st
holder.

FRONT
Work as for Back until armhole shaping is completed,
then cont without shaping
until armholes measure 14
(15, 16) cm/5$\frac{1}{2}$ (6, 6$\frac{1}{4}$)″, ending
with a WS row.

Shape neck
Next row: Patt 31 (32, 33),
turn and leave rem sts on
spare needle.
Dec one st at neck edge on
next 5 rows. 26 (27, 28) sts.
Cont without shaping until
armhole measures as for
Back, ending with a WS row.

Shape shoulders
Cast/bind off 9 sts at beg of
next and foll alt row.
Work 1 row, then cast/bind
off rem 8 (9, 10) sts.
Return to sts on spare needle,
sl first 19 (21, 23) sts on to st
holder for neck, rejoin yarn
and patt to end.
Cont to match first side.

SLEEVES
With 4$\frac{1}{2}$ mm/No 7 needles
and A, cast on 30 (34, 38) sts
and work 14 rows in k2, p2
rib as for Back, inc 9 sts
evenly across last row. 39
(43, 47) sts.
Change to 5$\frac{1}{2}$ mm/No 9
needles and cont in st st, inc
one st at each end of 11th
and every foll 6th row until
there are 61 (65, 69) sts.

Then cont without shaping
until sleeve measures 43 cm/
17″ from beg, ending with a p
row.

Shape top/cap
Cast/bind off 4 (5, 6) sts at
beg of next 2 rows.
Dec one st at each end of
next and every other row
until 37 sts rem, ending with
a p row.
Cast/bind off 2 sts at beg of
next 4 rows.
Cast/bind off rem 29 sts.

NECKBAND
Join left shoulder seam.
With 4$\frac{1}{2}$ mm/No 7 needles, A
and RS facing, k back neck
sts dec 5 sts evenly across
them, pick up and k17 (19,
21) sts down Left Front neck,
k front neck sts dec 3 sts
evenly across them, then
pick up and k17 (19, 21) sts
up Left Front neck. 74 (82,
90) sts.
Beg with a 2nd row, work 14
rows in rib as for Back.
Cast/bind off in rib.

ASSEMBLY
Press work according to in-
structions on yarn band.
Join right shoulder seam and
neckband. Sew in sleeves.
Join side and sleeve seams.
Fold neckband in half to in-
side and sew in place.
Press seams.

Pebble

MATERIALS
15 (17, 20, 23, 25, 27) 50 g/
1$\frac{3}{4}$ oz balls (each approx
125 m/137 yds) of Patons
Moorland Tweed (double
knitting/sport to knitting
worsted weight yarn)
1 pair each of 3$\frac{1}{4}$ mm/No 3
and 4 mm/No 6 knitting

needles
3 buttons

MEASUREMENTS
To fit 81 (86, 91, 97, 102,
107) cm/32 (34, 36, 38, 40,
42)″ bust or chest
Length 54 (57, 60, 63, 66, 69)
cm/21$\frac{1}{4}$ (22$\frac{1}{4}$, 23$\frac{3}{4}$, 24$\frac{3}{4}$, 26,
27)″
Sleeve seam 44 (46, 48, 50, 52,
54) cm/17$\frac{1}{4}$ (18, 19, 19$\frac{3}{4}$, 20$\frac{1}{2}$,
21$\frac{1}{4}$)″

TENSION/GAUGE
20 sts and 28 rows to 10 cm/
4″ over st st using 4 mm/No 6
needles.

BACK
With smaller needles, cast
on 85 (91, 97, 103, 109, 115)
sts.
1st row: K2, *p1, k1, rep
from * to last st, k1.
2nd row: K1, *p1, k1, rep
from * to end.
Rep these 2 rows 7 times
more, inc one st at end of last
row. 86 (92, 98, 104, 110, 116)
sts.
Change to larger needles and
beg patt as foll:
1st row: K4 (7, 10, 13, 16, 4);
k into front, back, front,
back then front of next st,
thus making 5 sts out of one
st, k next st, turn, p5, turn,
k5, turn, p5, turn, sl 2nd, 3rd,
4th and 5th sts over first st,
then k into back of first st
completing bobble – called
MB, *k13, MB, rep from *
until 5 (8, 11, 14, 17, 5) sts
rem, k to end.
2nd row: K1, p2 (5, 8, 11, 14,
2), k5, *p10, k5, rep from *
until 3 (6, 9, 12, 15, 3) sts rem,
p to last st, k1.
3rd row: K to end.
4th row: As 2nd row.
5th–8th rows: As 1st–4th
rows.
9th–11th rows: As 1st–3rd
rows.
12th row: K to end.
13th–16th rows: As 1st–4th
rows.
17th row: *K1, MB, rep from
* to last 2 sts, k2.
18th row: As 2nd row.
19th and 20th rows: K to
end.
Rep these 20 rows to form
patt.
Cont in patt until work measures 37 (39, 41, 42, 44, 46)
cm/14$\frac{1}{2}$ (15$\frac{1}{4}$, 16$\frac{1}{4}$, 16$\frac{1}{2}$, 17$\frac{1}{4}$,
18)″, ending with a WS row.

Shape armholes

Cast/bind off 4 sts at beg of next 2 rows, then dec one st at each end of every row until 66 (70, 72, 76, 78, 82) sts rem.

Cont in patt without shaping until armholes measure 17 (18, 19, 21, 22, 23) cm/6¾ (7, 7½, 8¼, 8¾, 9)″, ending with a WS row.

Shape shoulders
Cast/bind off 6 (7, 7, 8, 8, 9) sts at beg of next 4 rows and 7 sts at beg of next 2 rows. Break off yarn and leave rem 28 (28, 30, 30, 32, 32) sts on a spare needle.

FRONT
Work as for Back until work measures approx 30 (30, 30, 38, 38, 38) cm/12 (12, 12, 15, 15, 15)″, ending with a 20th patt row.

Divide for neck
Next row: Work 37 (40, 43, 46, 49, 52) sts, turn.
Cont on this set of sts for left side, working in patt without shaping until work measures as for Back to armholes.

Shape armhole
Cast/bind off 4 sts at beg of next row. Work 1 row.
Dec one st at side edge on every row until 27 (29, 30, 32, 33, 35) sts rem.
Cont in patt without shaping until armhole measures 8 (9, 10, 11, 12, 13) cm/3¼ (3½, 4, 4¼, 4¾, 5)″, ending with a WS row.

Shape neck
Dec one st at neck edge on next 3 rows, then on every RS row until 19 (21, 21, 23, 23, 25) sts rem.
Cont without shaping until armhole measures as for Back.

Shape shoulder
Cast/bind off 6 (7, 7, 8, 8, 9) sts at beg of next and foll alt row.
Work 1 row, cast/bind off rem 7 sts. Sl centre 12 sts at front on to st holder.
Join yarn to rem sts and complete right side to match left side, reversing shaping.

SLEEVES
Cast on 45 (45, 49, 49, 57, 57) sts with smaller needles.
Work 22 rows in rib as for Back, inc one st at each end of last row for 1st, 2nd, 5th and 6th sizes and inc 4 sts across last row for 3rd and

4th sizes. 47 (47, 53, 53, 59, 59) sts.
Change to larger needles and work in patt as foll:
1st row: K7 (7, 10, 10, 13, 13), MB, *k13, MB, rep from * to last 8 (8, 11, 11, 14, 14) sts, k to end.
2nd row: K1, p5 (5, 8, 8, 11, 11), k5, *p10, k5, rep from * to last 6 (6, 9, 9, 12, 12) sts rem, p to last st, k1.
3rd row: K to end.
4th row: As 2nd row.
5th–8th rows: As 1st–4th rows.
Working extra sts into patt to correspond with Back, inc one st at each end of next and every foll 8th row until there are 63 (67, 71, 75, 79, 83) sts.
Work in patt without shaping until work measures 44 (46, 48, 50, 52, 54) cm/17¼ (18, 19, 19¾, 20½, 21¼)″, or length required, ending with a WS row.

Shape top/cap
Cast/bind off 4 sts at beg·of next 2 rows.
Dec one st at each end of next and every other row until 35 (39, 43, 47, 51, 55) sts rem.
Work 1 row.
Dec one st at each end of every row until 15 sts rem. Cast/bind off.

BORDERS AND COLLAR
Join shoulder seams.

Lady's version
With smaller needles, cast on one st, then k first 3 sts from st holder at Centre Front, turn, cast on 6 sts.
Cont in g st on these 10 sts for Left Front border until work fits front opening as far as beg of neck shaping, ending with a WS row. Break off yarn and leave sts on a spare needle.
Mark position of 3 buttons, the first approx 5 cm/2″ from beg of opening, the last 3 cm/1¼″ from upper edge, and one midway between.
With smaller needles, k rem 9 sts from Centre Front, then cast on one st. Work right side to match left side, making 3 buttonholes when marked positions have been reached, as foll:
1st buttonhole row: K3, cast/bind off 2 sts, k to end.
2nd buttonhole row: K to end, casting on 2 sts over

those cast/bound off.
*With smaller needles, k the sts of Right Front border, pick up and k25 (25, 27, 27, 29, 29) sts along Right Front neck edge, k sts of back, pick up and k25 (25, 27, 27, 29, 29) sts along Left Front neck edge and k sts of Left Front border. 98 (98, 104, 104, 110, 110) sts.
Work 11 (11, 12, 12, 13, 13) cm/4¼ (4¼, 4¾, 4¾, 5, 5)″ in g st, ending with a RS row of collar. Cast/bind off.

Man's version
Sl first 9 sts of Centre Front on to a st holder.
With smaller needles, cast on 6 sts, k rem 3 sts of Centre Front, then cast on one st.
Cont in g st on these 10 sts for Right Front border until work fits front opening as far as beg of neck shaping, ending with a WS row. Leave sts on a spare needle but do not break off yarn.
Mark position of 3 buttons as for lady's version.
With smaller needles and new yarn, cast on one st, then k9 sts of Left Front.
Work to match RS, making 3 buttonholes when marked positions have been reached as foll:
1st buttonhole row: K to last 5 sts, cast/bind off 2 sts, k to end.
2nd buttonhole row: K to end, casting on 2 sts over those cast/bound off.
Break off yarn.
Return to sts of Right Front and work collar as for lady's version from * to end.

ASSEMBLY
Join side and sleeve seams.
Set in sleeves.
Sew borders to edges of opening and sew button side in position under buttonhole side at base.
Press seams lightly under a damp cloth.
Sew on buttons.

Lace

MATERIALS

8 (9) 50 g/1¾ oz balls (each approx 99 m/108 yds) of Robin *Thermospun* (chunky/bulky weight yarn)

1 pair each of 4½ mm/No 7 and 5½ mm/No 9 knitting needles

Approx 1 m/1 yd of 6 cm/2½″ wide cotton lace elasticated along inner edge

MEASUREMENTS

To fit 86–91 (91–97) cm/34–36 (36–38)″ bust

Length 58 (61) cm/22¾ (24)″

Sleeve seam 48 cm/19″

TENSION/GAUGE

16 sts and 20 rows to 10 cm/4″ over patt using 5½ mm/No 9 needles.

Note: The number of sts varies throughout the pattern, always count them after a WS row.

BACK

With smaller needles, cast on 75 (83) sts and work in k1, p1 rib for 8 cm/3¼″, ending with a WS row and inc one st in last row. 76 (84) sts.

Change to larger needles and cont in patt as foll:

1st row: (RS) K2, *yfwd/yo, k1 tbl, yfwd/yo, sl 1–k1–. psso, k5, rep from * to last 2 sts, k2.

2nd row: P6, *p2 tog tbl, p7, rep from * to last 7 sts, p2 tog tbl, p5.

3rd row: K2, *yfwd/yo, k1 tbl, yfwd/yo, k2, sl 1–k1–psso, k3, rep from * to last 2 sts, k2.

4th row: P4, *p2 tog tbl, p7, rep from * to end.

5th row: K2, *k1 tbl, yfwd/yo, k4, sl 1–k1–psso, k1, yfwd/yo, rep from * to last 2

sts, k2.

6th row: P3, *p2 tog tbl, p7, rep from * to last st, p1.

7th row: K2, *k5, k2 tog, yfwd/yo, k1 tbl, yfwd/yo, rep from * to last 2 sts, k2.

8th row: P5, *p2 tog, p7, rep from * to last 8 sts, p2 tog, p6.

9th row: K2, *k3, k2 tog, k2, yfwd/yo, k1 tbl, yfwd/yo, rep from * to last 2 sts, k2.

10th row: *P7, p2 tog, rep from * to last 4 sts, p4.

11th row: K2, *yfwd/yo, k1, k2 tog, k4, yfwd/yo, k1 tbl, rep from * to last 2 sts, k2.

12th row: P1, *p7, p2 tog, rep from * to last 3 sts, p3.

Rep these 12 rows until work measures 37 (38) cm/14½ (15)″ from beg, ending with a WS row.

Shape armholes

Keeping patt correct, cast/bind off 8 sts at beg of next row and 9 sts at beg of foll row. 60 (68) sts.

Cont without shaping until armholes measure 21 (23) cm/8¼ (9)″, ending with a WS row.

Next row: Cast/bind off 18 (22) sts, patt to end.

Next row: Cast/bind off 18 (22) sts, plus extra sts made in patt, then patt to end.

Leave rem 24 sts on st holder.

FRONT

Work as for Back until armholes measure 12 (13) cm/4¾ (5)″, ending with a WS row.

Shape neck

Next row: Keeping patt correct, patt 26 (30), turn and leave rem sts on spare needle. Work 2 rows.

Cast/bind off 9 sts at beg of next row, then cont on rem 18 (22) sts until armhole measures as for Back, ending with a WS row.

Cast/bind off.

Return to sts on spare needle, leave centre 8 sts on spare needle, rejoin yarn and patt to end.

Work 1 row.

Cast/bind off 8 sts at beg of next row, then cont to match first side.

SLEEVES

With smaller needles, cast on 41 (47) sts and work in k1, p1 rib for 8 cm/3¼″, ending with an RS row.

Next row: Rib 2 (3), *inc in next st, rib 1, rep from * to last 1 (2) sts, rib 1 (2). 60 (68)

sts.

Change to larger needles and cont in patt as for Back until sleeve measures 48 cm/19″ from beg, ending with a WS row.

Place marker at each end of last row, then work a further 5 cm/2″.

Cast/bind off loosely.

NECKBAND

Join left shoulder seam.

With smaller needles and RS facing, k back neck sts, inc 7 sts evenly across them, pick up and k19 (21) sts down Left Front neck, k front neck sts, then pick up and k19 (21) sts up Right Front neck. 77 (81) sts.

Beg next row with p1, work 6 rows in k1, p1 rib.

Cast/bind off in rib.

ASSEMBLY

Do not press.

Join right shoulder seam and neckband.

Sew in sleeves, sewing last part of sleeve seams to cast/bound-off sts at armholes.

Join side and sleeve seams.

Sew elasticated edge of lace inside neckband, joining ends of lace at shoulder seam.

Coconut

MATERIALS

7 (8, 8, 9) 25 g/1 oz balls (each approx 102 m/112 yds) of Lister–Lee *St Tropez* (light weight novelty bouclé) in main colour (M)

1 (1, 1, 2) 50 g/1¾ oz balls (each approx 183 m/200 yds) of Lister–Lee *Motoravia 4 ply* (4 ply/fingering to sport weight yarn) in contrast colour (C)

1 pair each of 2¾ mm/No 2 and 3¾ mm/No 5 knitting needles

Set of four 2¾ mm/No 2 double-pointed knitting needles

MEASUREMENTS

To fit 81 (86, 91, 97) cm/32 (34, 36, 38)″ bust

Length 55 (56, 57, 58) cm/21¾ (22¼, 22½, 23)″

Sleeve seam 32 cm/12½″

TENSION/GAUGE

22 sts and 32 rows to 10 cm/4″ over st st using 3¾ mm/No 5 needles and M.

BACK

With smaller needles and C, cast on 93 (99, 105, 111) sts.

1st row: K1, *p1, k1, rep from * to end.

2nd row: P1, *k1, p1, rep from * to end.

Rep these 2 rows for 6 cm/2½″, ending with a WS row. Break off C.

Change to larger needles, join in M and beg with a k row, cont in st st until work measures 36 cm/14¼″ from beg, ending with a p row.

Shape armholes

Cast/bind off 5 sts at beg of next 2 rows. 83 (89, 95, 101) sts.

Cont without shaping until armholes measure 19 (20, 21, 22) cm/7½ (8, 8¼, 8¾)″, ending with a p row.

Shape shoulders

Cast/bind off 17 (20, 23, 26) sts at beg of next 2 rows.

Leave rem 49 sts on st holder.

FRONT

Work as for Back until armholes measure 11 (12, 13, 14) cm/4½ (4¾, 5, 5½)″, ending with a p row.

Shape neck

Next row: K27 (30, 33, 36), turn and leave rem sts on spare needle.

Dec one st at neck edge on every other row until 17 (20, 23, 26) sts rem, then cont without shaping until armhole measures as for Back, ending with a p row.

Cast/bind off.

Return to sts on spare needle, sl first 29 sts on to st holder for neck, rejoin yarn and k to end. Cont to match first side.

SLEEVES

With smaller needles and C, cast on 63 (67, 71, 75) sts and work in rib as for Back for 12 cm/4¾″, ending with a

WS row.
Break off C.
Change to larger needles, join in M and beg with a k row, cont in st st, inc one st at each end of next and every foll 4th row until there are 85 (89, 93, 97) sts, then cont without shaping until sleeve measures 34 cm/13½" from beg, ending with a p row.
Cast/bind off.

NECKBAND

Join shoulder seams.
With set of four double-pointed needles and C, k back neck sts, pick up and k26 sts down Left Front neck, k front neck sts, then pick up and k26 sts up Right Front neck. 130 sts.
Work in rounds of k1, p1 rib for 2 cm/¾".

ASSEMBLY

Do not press.
Sew in sleeves, sewing last 2 cm/¾" of sleeve seams to cast/bound-off sts at arm-holes.
Join side and sleeve seams; reversing seam on cuff to fold in half to RS if required.

Oats

MATERIALS

8 (9, 9, 10) 100 g/3½ oz balls (each approx 130 m/142 yds) of Twilleys *Pegasus* (medium weight cotton)
1 pair each of 4½ mm/No 7 and 5 mm/No 8 knitting needles
5.00 mm/size H crochet hook
6 buttons

MEASUREMENTS

To fit 97 (102, 107, 112) cm/ 38 (40, 42, 44)" chest
Length 56 (58, 61, 66) cm/22 (22¾, 24, 26)"
Sleeve seam 46 (47, 48, 53) cm/18 (18½, 19, 21)"

TENSION/GAUGE

17 sts and 26 rows to 10 cm/4" over patt using 5 mm/No 8 needles.

BACK

With smaller needles, cast on 85 (91, 97, 103) sts and work in rib as foll:
1st row: *K1, p1, rep from * to last st, k1.
2nd row: *P1, k1, rep from * to last st, p1.
Rep these 2 rows 5 (5, 5, 7) times more.
Change to larger needles and work in diamond patt as foll:
1st row: (RS) *P1, k5, rep from * to last st, p1.
2nd row: P1, k1, *p3, k1, p1, k1, rep from * to last 5 sts, p3, k1, p1.
3rd row: K2, *p1, k1, p1, k3, rep from * to last 5 sts, p1, k1, p1, k2.
4th row: P3, *k1, p5, rep from * to last 4 sts, k1, p3.
5th row: As 3rd row.
6th row: As 2nd row.
These 6 rows form diamond patt. Cont in patt until work measures 11 (11, 11, 13) cm/ 4¼ (4¼, 4¼, 5)" from beg inc 1 st at each end of last row. Cont in patt without shaping until work measures 33 (33, 33, 36) cm/13 (13, 13, 14¼)" from beg, inc 1 st at each end of last row on 1st, 2nd and 3rd sizes only. 89 (95, 101, 105) sts.
Cont in patt without shaping until work measures 37 (38, 40, 43) cm/14½ (15, 15¾, 17)".
Place a marker at each end of next row to mark beg of armholes.
Cont in patt until work measures 56 (58, 61, 66) cm/22 (22¾, 24, 26)" from beg, ending with a WS row.

Shape shoulders

Cast/bind off 8 sts at beg of next 6 rows and 2 (4, 6, 7) sts at beg of next 2 rows.
Cast/bind off rem 37 (39, 41, 43) sts.

FRONT

Work as for Back until work measures 55 (56, 58, 62) cm/ 21½ (22, 22¾, 24½)", ending with a WS row.

Shape neck

Next row: Patt 32 (34, 36, 38) sts, turn and leave rem sts on spare needle.
Dec one st at neck edge on next 6 (6, 6, 7) rows, and AT THE SAME TIME when work measures as for Back to shoulder, ending at arm-hole edge, shape shoulder by casting/binding off 8 sts at armhole edge on next and foll 2 alt rows and 2 (4, 6, 7) sts at armhole edge on foll alt row. Fasten off.
Rejoin yarn to rem 57 (61, 65, 67) sts and cast/bind off centre 25 (27, 29, 29) sts, then work rem 32 (34, 36, 38) sts to match first side.

SLEEVES

With smaller needles, cast on 43 (49, 49, 55) sts and work 11 (11, 11, 13) cm/4¼ (4¼, 4¼, 5)" in k1, p1 rib as for Back, ending with a 2nd rib row.
Change to larger needles and work in patt as for Back, inc one st at each end of every 4th (6th, 4th, 6th) row until there are 79 (79, 85, 89) sts.
Cont without shaping until sleeve measures 46 (47, 48, 53) cm/18 (18½, 19, 21)" from beg.
Cast/bind off loosely.

COLLAR

Join left shoulder seam.
With RS facing and smaller needles, pick up and k37 (39, 41, 43) sts from back neck edge and 54 (56, 58, 66) sts around front neck edge. 91 (95, 99, 109) sts. Work 18 (18, 18, 20) cm/7 (7, 7, 7¾)" in k1, p1 rib as for Back.
Cast/bind off loosely in rib.

ASSEMBLY

Join right shoulder seam for 2.5 cm/1" from armhole edge.
Set sleeves into armholes.
Join side and sleeve seams.
With RS facing, work one row of dc/sc along open shoulder seam of back and side edge of collar. Fasten off.
With RS facing, work one row of dc/sc along side edge of collar and open seam of front shoulder, then work one row of dc/sc on dc/sc, making 6 buttonholes by working 2ch, miss/skip 2dc/ sc at equal intervals. Fasten off.
Sew 4 buttons to RS of shoulder and collar and rem 2 buttons to inside of collar so that buttons show when collar is folded back and fastened.
Press seams lightly on WS.

Ribbed Sweater

MATERIALS
8 (8, 9) 50 g/1¾ oz balls (each approx 119 m/130 yds) of Sirdar *Majestic DK* (double knitting/knitting worsted weight yarn) in main colour (M)

2 (2, 3) 25 g/1 oz balls (each approx 47 m/51 yds) of Sirdar *Nocturne* (medium weight mohair) in contrast colour (C)

1 pair each of 3¾ mm/No 5 and 6 mm/No 10 knitting needles

2 buttons

MEASUREMENTS
To fit 86 (91, 97) cm/34 (36, 38)″ bust

Length 57 (58, 59) cm/22½ (23, 23½)″

Sleeve seam 52 cm/20½″

TENSION/GAUGE
23 sts and 23 rows to 10 cm/4″ over twisted rib patt using 6 mm/No 10 needles and M.

BACK
With smaller needles and M, cast on 99 (105, 111) sts. Beg twisted rib as foll:

1st row: P1, *knit through back loop of next st (called k1b), p1, rep from * to end.

2nd row: K1b, *p1, k1b, rep from * to end.

Rep these 2 rows for twisted rib patt for 9 cm/3½″, ending with a 2nd row.

Change to larger needles, join in C.

Next row: *Sl 1, k1, yfwd/yo to make 1, psso the k st and the made st, rep from * to last st, k1.

Next row: P to end.

Rep these 2 rows twice more. Break off C.

Using M, cont in twisted rib patt until work measures 36 cm/14¼″ from beg, ending with a WS row.

Shape armholes
Cast/bind off 4 sts at beg of next 2 rows, 2 sts at beg of next 2 rows, then dec one st at each end of next and foll 3 (4, 5) alt rows. 79 (83, 87) sts. Cont without shaping until armholes measure 13 (14, 15) cm/5 (5½, 6)″, ending with a WS row.

Break off M, join in C and cont in patt as above waist rib for 8 cm/3¼″, ending with a WS row.

Cast/bind off loosely.

FRONT
Work as for Back until work measures 36 cm/14¼″ from beg, but ending with a RS row – one row less than for Back.

Shape armholes and divide for neck
Next row: Patt 44 (47, 50), cast/bind off 11 sts, patt to end. Cont on last 44 (47, 50) sts, cast/bind off 4 sts at beg of next row, 2 sts at beg of foll alt row, then dec one st at beg of foll 4 (5, 6) alt rows. 34 (36, 38) sts.

Cont without shaping until armhole measures 13 (14, 15) cm/5 (5½, 6)″, ending with a WS row.

Break off M, join in C and cont in patt as for Back for 8 cm/3¼″ omitting a k1 at end of RS rows, ending with a WS row.

Cast/bind off.

Return to other 44 (47, 50) sts and work to match, reversing shaping.

SLEEVES
With larger needles and M, cast on 11 (15, 19) sts and beg at top of sleeve. Work 2 rows in twisted rib patt, then cont in patt, cast on 10 sts at beg of next 8 rows. 91 (95, 99) sts.

Cont in patt, dec one st at each end of 5th and every foll 6th row until 63 (67, 71) sts rem, then cont without shaping until edge of sleeve measures 40 cm/15¾″, ending with a RS row.

Next row: Patt to end, dec 6 (8, 10) sts evenly across row.

Join in C and work 6 rows in patt as above waist rib on Back.

Break off C.

Change to smaller needles and cont in M, working in twisted rib for 9 cm/3½″.

Cast/bind off loosely in rib.

RIGHT FRONT COLLAR
With smaller needles and M, cast on 15 sts and work in twisted rib patt as for Back for 5 cm/2″, ending with a 2nd row.

Next row: Rib 4, work twice into next st, rib to end.

Next row: Rib to last 6 sts, [k1b] twice, [p1, k1b] twice.

Next row: Rib 4, work twice into next st, rib to end.

Next row: Rib to end as 2nd patt row. Rep these 4 rows 7 times more. 31 sts. Then cont in rib until straight edge measures same as front neck edge of sweater, ending with a WS row.

Cast/bind off in rib.

LEFT FRONT COLLAR
With smaller needles and M, cast on 15 sts and work in twisted rib patt as for Back for 5 cm/2″, ending with a 2nd row.

Next row: Rib to last 5 sts, work twice into next st, rib 4.

Next row: [K1b, p1] twice, [k1b] twice, rib to end.

Next row: Rib to last 5 sts, work twice into next st, rib 4.

Next row: Rib to end as 2nd patt row. Cont to match Right Front Collar.

BACK COLLAR
With smaller needles and M, cast on 39 sts and work in twisted rib patt as for Back for 5 cm/2″, ending with a 2nd row.

Next row: Rib 4, work twice into next st, rib to last 5 sts, work twice into next st, rib 4.

Cont to inc at each end of every other row until there are 71 sts, ending with a WS row.

Cast/bind off in rib.

ASSEMBLY
Do not press.

Join shoulder seams for 24 (26, 28) sts from shoulder edge.

Sew on 2 front sections of collar sewing straight side edge to neck edge and overlapping right over left at lower edge of opening. Sew cast on edge of back collar to neck edge, sew sides to the rem part of front shoulders which were left open and to cast/bound-off edges of front collar sections.

Sew in sleeves. Join side and sleeve seams.

Sew 2 buttons to Left Front and make loops on Right Front as in picture.

Fair Isle Slipover

MATERIALS
3 (3, 4, 4) 50 g/1¾ oz balls (each approx 200 m/220 yds) of Pingouin *Pingolaine/Mohair 50* (3 ply/fingering weight yarn) in main colour (M)

1 (1, 2, 2) balls in 1st contrast colour (A)

1 ball in each of 5 contrast colours (B, C, D, E and F)

1 50 g/1¾ oz ball (each approx 120 m/130 yds) of Pingouin *Laine et Mohair/Mohair 50* (light weight mohair) in each of 4 contrast colours (G, H, I, J)

1 pair each of 2¾ mm/No 2 and 3 mm/No 3 knitting needles

Set of four 2¾ mm/No 2 double-pointed knitting needles

Embroidery needle

MEASUREMENTS
To fit 81–86 (86–91, 91–97, 96–102) cm/32–34 (34–36, 36–38, 38–40)″ bust

Length 54 (55, 57, 58) cm/21¼ (21¾, 22½, 22¾)″

TENSION/GAUGE
31 sts and 34 rows to 10 cm/4″ over patt using 3 mm/No 3 needles

BACK
With smaller needles and M, cast on 127 (135, 143, 151) sts.

1st row: P1, *k1, p1, rep

from * to end.

2nd row: K1, *p1, k1, rep from * to end.

Rep these 2 rows 6 times more, inc 12 sts evenly across last row. 139 (147, 155, 163) sts.

Beg with a k row, work 2 rows in st st.

Change to larger needles and cont in st st, working in patt from chart reading odd numbered rows from right to left and even rows from left to right.

Cont in patt until work measures 34 (34, 35, 35) cm/$13\frac{1}{2}$ ($13\frac{1}{2}$, $13\frac{3}{4}$, $13\frac{3}{4}$)″, ending with a p row.

Shape armholes

Keeping patt correct, cast/

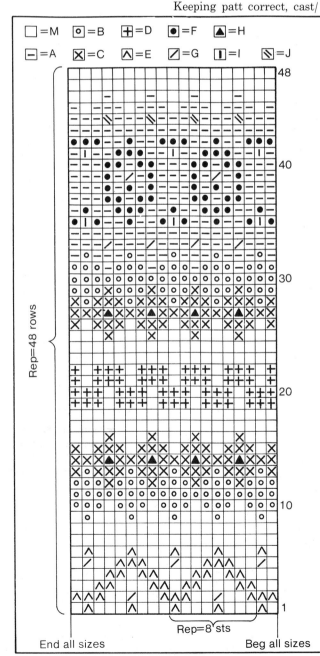

□=M ⊙=B ⊞=D ⦿=F ▲=H

−=A ⊠=C ⋀=E ⃫=G ⫾=I ⃰=J

Rep=48 rows

48
40
30
20
10
1

Rep=8 sts

End all sizes   Beg all sizes

Fairisle chart, worked in stocking/stockingette stitch.

bind off 4 sts at beg of next 2 rows**, 2 sts at beg of next 8 (10, 10, 12) rows, then dec one st at each end of next and foll 3 (3, 5, 5) alt rows. 107 (111, 115, 119) sts.

Cont without shaping until armholes measure 20 (21, 22, 23) cm/$7\frac{3}{4}$ ($8\frac{1}{4}$, $8\frac{3}{4}$, 9)″, ending with a p row.

Shape shoulders and neck

Cast/bind off 7 (7, 8, 8) sts at beg of next 2 rows.

Next row: Cast/bind off 7 (7, 8, 8) sts, k24 (26, 25, 27) including st on needle, turn and leave rem sts on spare needle.

Next row: Cast/bind off 5 sts, p to end.

Next row: Cast/bind off 7 (7, 8, 8) sts, k to end.

Next row: Cast/bind off 5 sts, p to end.

Cast/bind off rem 7 (9, 7, 9) sts.

Return to sts on spare needle, sl first 31 (31, 33, 33) sts on st holder for neck, rejoin yarn and k to end.

Cont to match first side, reversing shaping.

FRONT

Work as for Back to **. 131 (147, 155) sts.

Divide for neck

Next row: Cast/bind off 2 sts, k63 (67, 71, 75) including st on needle, turn and leave rem sts on spare needle.

Cont to cast/bind off 2 sts at armhole edge on next 3 (4, 4, 5) alt rows, then dec one st at beg of foll 4 (4, 6, 6) alt rows, and AT THE SAME TIME dec one st at neck edge on every other row 15 (13, 11, 9) times, then on every 3rd row until 28 (30, 31, 33) sts rem.

Cont without shaping until armhole measures as for Back, ending with a p row.

Shape shoulder

Cast/bind off 7 (7, 8, 8) sts at beg of next and foll 2 alt rows.

P 1 row, then cast/bind off rem 7 (9, 7, 9) sts.

Return to sts on spare needle, sl first st on to st holder for neck, rejoin yarn and k to end.

Cont to match first side, reversing all shaping.

NECKBAND

Join shoulder seams.

With set of four double-

pointed needles and M, pick up and k51 (51, 53, 53) sts around back neck including sts on st holder, 69 (72, 75, 78) sts down Left Front neck, k Centre Front st from st holder, then pick up and k69 (72, 75, 78) sts up Right Front neck.

Next round: Work in k1, p1 rib to 2 sts before Centre Front, k2 tog, p1, k2 tog tbl, rib to end.

Rep this round 9 times more, then cast/bind off in rib, still dec at front.

ARMHOLE BORDERS

With smaller needles and M, pick up and k147 (153, 159, 165) sts around armhole and work 10 rows in rib as at beg. Cast/bind off in rib.

ASSEMBLY

Press work according to instructions on yarn band.
Join side seams.
Press seams.

Soft Diamonds

MATERIALS

5 (6) 25 g/1 oz balls (each approx 59 m/65 yds) of Jaeger *Mohair-spun* (medium weight mohair) in main colour (M)

2 balls in first contrast colour (A)

2 (3) balls in 2nd contrast colour (B)

4 balls in 3rd contrast colour (C)

1 pair each of $4\frac{1}{2}$ mm/No 7 and $5\frac{1}{2}$ mm/No 9 knitting needles

Set of four $4\frac{1}{2}$ mm/No 7 double-pointed knitting needles

MEASUREMENTS

To fit 81–86 (89–94) cm/32–34 (35–37)″ bust

Length 54 (57) cm/$21\frac{1}{4}$ ($22\frac{1}{2}$)″

TENSION/GAUGE

20 sts and approx 20 rows to 10 cm/4″ over patt using 5½ mm/No 9 needles.

BACK

With smaller needles and M, cast on 75 (83) sts.

1st row: P1, *k1, p1, rep from * to end.

2nd row: K1, *p1, k1, rep from * to end.

Rep these 2 rows for 9 cm/3½″, ending with a RS row.

Next row: P5 (9), *[inc in next st, p4] 13 times, inc in next st, p to end. 89 (97) sts.

Change to larger needles and cont in st st, working in patt as foll: (**Note:** Strand yarns loosely at back of work, weaving in if carried over more than 5 sts.)

1st row: K4C, *1A, 7C, rep from * to last 5 sts, 1A, 4C.

2nd row: P3C, *3A, 5C, rep from * to last 6 sts, 3A, 3C.

3rd row: K2C, *5A, 3C, rep from * to last 7 sts, 5A, 2C.

4th row: P1C, *7A, 1C, rep from * to end.

5th row: As 3rd row.

6th row: As 2nd row.

7th row: As 1st row.

8th row: P in C.

9th–16th rows: As 1st–8th rows, but using B instead of A.

17th–24th rows: As 1st–8th rows, but using M instead of A.

Rep these 24 rows until work measures 33 cm/13″ from beg, ending with a p row.

Shape armholes

Keeping patt correct, cast/bind off 6 sts at beg of next 2 rows. 77 (85) sts.**

Cont without shaping until armholes measure 21 (24) cm/8¼ (9½)″, ending with a p row.

Shape shoulders

Cast/bind off 8 (9) sts at beg of next 4 rows, then 9 (10) sts at beg of next 2 rows.

Leave rem 27 (29) sts on st holder.

FRONT

Work as for Back to **, then cont without shaping until armholes measure 4 (5) cm/1½ (2)″, ending with a p row.

Divide for neck

Next row: K38 (42), turn and leave rem sts on spare needle.

Dec one st at neck edge on

every other row until 25 (28) sts rem, then cont without shaping until armhole measures same as for Back, ending with a p row.

Shape shoulder

Cast/bind off 8 (9) sts at beg of next and foll alt row. P 1 row, then cast/bind off rem 9 (10) sts.

Return to sts on spare needle, sl first st on to st holder for neck, rejoin yarn and k to end.

Cont to match first side.

NECKBAND

Join shoulder seams. With set of four double-pointed needles, M and RS facing, k back neck sts, dec 4 sts across them, pick up and k32 (35) sts down Left Front neck, k Centre Front st, then pick up and k32 (35) sts up Right Front neck.

Next round: Work in k1, p1 rib to 2 sts before Centre Front, p2 tog, k1, p2 tog tbl, rib to end.

Rep this round 5 times more. Cast/bind off in rib, still dec at Centre Front.

ARMHOLE BORDERS

With smaller needles, M and RS facing, beg at inside of cast/bound-off sts at armholes and pick up and k73 (79) sts along armhole edge, ending at inside of cast/bound-off sts. Work 6 rows in rib as for Back.

Cast/bind off in rib.

ASSEMBLY

Do not press.

Join side seams. Sew ends of armhole borders to cast/bound-off sts at underarms.

MATERIALS

11 (11, 12, 13, 14, 15) 50 g/

1¾ oz balls (each approx 128 m/140 yds) of Twilleys *Stalite* (light weight cotton)

1 pair each of 2¾ mm/No 2 and 3¼ mm/No 3 knitting needles

Set of four 2¾ mm/No 2 double-pointed knitting needles

1 cable needle (cn)

MEASUREMENTS

To fit 81 (86, 91, 97, 102, 107) cm/32 (34, 36, 38, 40, 42)″ bust or chest

Length 63 (63, 66, 66, 69, 69) cm/24¾ (24¾, 26, 26, 27¼, 27¼)″

Sleeve seam 48 (48, 50, 50, 52, 52) cm/19 (19, 19¾, 19¾, 20½, 20½)″

TENSION/GAUGE

24 sts and 32 rows to 10 cm/4″ over st st using 3¼ mm/No 3 needles.

ABBREVIATIONS

cr5 = sl next 2 sts on to cn and hold at front of work, k2, p1, then k2 from cn.

cr3R = sl next st on to cn and hold at back of work, k2, then p1 from cn.

cr3L = sl next 2 sts to cn and hold at front of work, p1, then k2 from cn.

c6B = sl 3 sts to cn and hold at back of work, k3, then k3 from cn.

c6F = sl 3 sts to cn and hold at front of work, k3, then k3 from cn.

BACK

With smaller needles, cast on 103 (107, 113, 117, 123, 127) sts.

1st row: K1, *p1, k1, rep from * to end.

2nd row: P1, *k1, p1, rep from * to end.

Rep these 2 rows for 5 cm/2″, ending with a 1st row.

Next row: Rib 3 (1, 3, 1, 3, 1), *inc in next st, rib 4, rep from * to last 5 (1, 5, 1, 5, 1) sts, inc in next st, rib 4 (0, 4, 0, 4, 0). 123 (129, 135, 141, 147, 153) sts.

Change to larger needles and cont in patt as foll:

1st row: K9 (11, 13, 15, 17, 19), *p2, k6, p6, cr5, p6, k6, p2*, k39 (41, 43, 45, 47, 49), rep from * to *, k to end.

2nd row: P9 (11, 13, 15, 17, 19), *k2, p6, k6, p2, k1, p2, k6, p6, k2*, p39 (41, 43, 45, 47, 49), rep from * to *, p to end.

3rd row: K9 (11, 13, 15, 17, 19), *p2, c6B, p5, cr3R, k1, cr3L, p5, c6F, p2*, k39 (41, 43, 45, 47, 49), rep from * to *, k to end.

4th row: K9 (11, 13, 15, 17, 19), *k2, p6, k5, p2, k1, p1, k1, p2, k5, p6, k2*, k39 (41, 43, 45, 47, 49), rep from * to *, k to end.

5th row: P9 (11, 13, 15, 17, 19), *p2, k6, p4, cr3R, k1, p1, k1, cr3L, p4, k6, p2*, p39 (41, 43, 45, 47, 49), rep from * to *, p to end.

6th row: K9 (11, 13, 15, 17, 19), *k2, p6, k4, p2, k1, [p1, k1] twice, p2, k4, p6, k2*, k39 (41, 43, 45, 47, 49), rep from * to *, k to end.

These 6 rows form the rep of ridge patt at each end and in centre. Keeping these sts correct, cont with panels as foll:

7th row: *p2, k6, p3, cr3R, k1, [p1, k1] twice, cr3L, p3, k6, p2*.

8th row: *k2, p6, k3, p2, k1, [p1, k1] 3 times, p2, k3, p6, k2*.

9th row: *p2, c6B, p2, cr3R, k1, [p1, k1] 3 times, cr3L, p2, c6F, p2*.

10th row: *k2, p6, k2, p2, k1, [p1, k1] 4 times, p2, k2, p6, k2*.

11th row: *p2, k6, p2, cr3L, p1, [k1, p1] 3 times, cr3R, p2, k6, p2*.

12th row: As 8th row.

13th row: *p2, k6, p3, cr3L, p1, [k1, p1] twice, cr3R, p3, k6, p2*.

14th row: As 6th row.

15th row: *p2, c6B, p4, cr3L, p1, k1, p1, cr3R, p4, c6F, p2*.

16th row: As 4th row.

17th row: *p2, k6, p5, cr3L, p1, cr3R, p5, k6, p2*.

18th row: As 2nd row.

These 18 rows form the rep of patt for Aran panels. Keeping all patts correct, cont until work measures 43 (43, 44, 44, 45, 45) cm/17 (17, 17¼, 17¼, 17¾, 17¾)″ from beg, ending with a WS row.

Shape armholes

Cast/bind off 4 sts at beg of next 2 rows. 115 (121, 127, 133, 139, 145) sts.

Cont without shaping until armholes measure 20 (20, 22, 22, 24, 24) cm/7¾ (7¾, 8¾, 8¾, 9½, 9½)″, ending with a WS row.

Shape shoulders

Cast/bind off 39 (42, 44, 47, 49, 52) sts loosely at beg of next 2 rows.

Leave rem 37 (37, 39, 39, 41, 41) sts on st holder.

FRONT

Work as for Back until work measures 40 (40, 41, 41, 42, 42) cm/15¾ (15¾, 16¼, 16¼, 16½, 16½)″ from beg, ending with a WS row.

Divide for neck

Next row: Patt 61 (64, 67, 70, 73, 76), turn and leave rem sts on spare needle.
Next row: Patt to end.
Next row: Patt to last 3 sts, k2 tog, k1.
Work 7 rows, dec 1 at neck edge on 4th of these rows.

Shape armhole

Next row: Cast/bind off 4 sts, patt to last 3 sts, k2 tog, k1.
Cont to dec 1 at neck edge on every 4th row until 39 (42, 44, 47, 49, 52) sts rem, then cont without shaping until armhole measures as for Back, ending with a WS row.
Cast/bind off loosely.
Return to sts on spare needle, sl first st on to st holder for neck, rejoin yarn and patt to end.
Next row: Patt to end.
Next row: K1, sl 1–k1–psso, patt to end.
Cont to match first side.

SLEEVES

With smaller needles, cast on 47 (47, 49, 49, 53, 53) sts and work in rib as for Back for 5 cm/2″, ending with a 1st row.
Next row: Rib 2 (2, 1, 1, 3, 3), *inc in next st, rib 1, rep from * to last 3 (3, 2, 2, 4) sts, inc in next st, rib 2 (2, 1, 1, 3, 3). 69 (69, 73, 73, 77, 77) sts.
Change to larger needles and cont in patt as foll:
1st row: K18 (18, 20, 20, 22, 22), work from * to * on 1st patt row of Back, k to end.
2nd row: P18 (18, 20, 20, 22, 22), work from * to * on 2nd patt row of Back, p to end.
Keeping the Aran panel in centre correct as for Back and sts at each end in 6-row ridge patt, inc one st at each end of 7th and every foll 6th row until there are 105 (105, 113, 113, 121, 121) sts, then cont without shaping until sleeve measures 50 (50, 52, 52, 54, 54) cm/19¾ (19¾, 20½, 20½, 21¼, 21¼)″ from beg, ending with a WS row.
Cast/bind off loosely.

NECKBAND

Join shoulder seams. With set of four double-pointed needles and RS facing, k back neck sts, pick up and k68 (68, 72, 72, 76, 76) sts down Left Front neck, k Centre Front st, then pick up and k68 (68, 72, 72, 76, 76) sts up Right Front neck.
Next round: Work in k1, p1 rib to 2 sts before Centre Front, p2 tog, k1, p2 tog tbl, rib to end.
Rep this round 6 times more. Cast/bind off in rib, still dec at Centre Front.

ASSEMBLY

Do not press, as it will flatten the pattern.
Sew in sleeves, sewing the last 2 cm/¾″ of sleeve seams to the cast/bound-off sts at armholes.
Join side and sleeve seams.

Fairisle Cardigan

MATERIALS

8 (8, 9) 40 g/1½ oz balls (each approx 85 m/95 yds) of Pingouin *Mohair/Mohair 50* (medium weight mohair) in main colour (M)
1 ball in each of 2 contrast colours (A and B)
1 pair each of 4½ mm/No 7 and 5 mm/No 8 knitting needles
4 buttons

MEASUREMENTS

To fit 81–86 (91–97, 102–107) cm/32–34 (36–38, 40–42)″ bust or chest
Length 56 (58, 60) cm/22 (22¾, 23½)″
Sleeve seam 44 (45, 46) cm/17¼ (17½, 18)″

TENSION/GAUGE

17 sts and 23 rows to 10 cm/4″ over st st using 5 mm/No 8 needles.

BACK

With smaller needles and M, cast on 78 (82, 90) sts.
1st row: K2, *p2, k2, rep from * to end.
2nd row: P2, *k2, p2, rep from * to end.
Rep these 2 rows 6 times more, inc 7 (9, 7) sts evenly in last row. 85 (91, 97) sts.
Change to larger needles and beg with a k row, cont in st st and work 24 rows of patt from chart, beg with chart row 1 and reading odd numbered rows from right to left and even rows from left to right.
Then cont in M until work measures 30 cm/11¾″ from beg, ending with a p row.
Work 1st–14th rows of chart.

Shape armholes

Still working in patt, cast/bind off 3 sts at beg of next 2 rows.
Dec one st at each end of

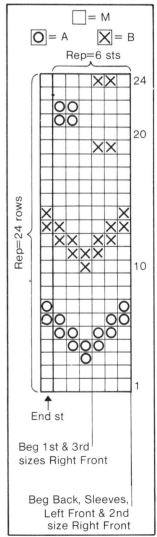

Fairisle chart

next and every other row until 33 (35, 37) sts rem, ending with a p row, but AT THE SAME TIME complete 24 rows of patt from chart, work 6 rows in M, work 19th–24th rows of patt from chart, then cont in M to end. Cast/bind off.

LEFT FRONT
With smaller needles and M, cast on 46 (46, 50) sts.
For woman's version: Work 13 rows in rib as for Back.
For man's version: Work 6 rows in rib as for Back.
7th row: Rib to last 7 sts, cast/bind off 2 sts, rib to end.
8th row: Rib 5, cast on 2 sts, rib to end.
Work 5 more rows in rib.

For both versions:
14th row: Rib 12 and sl these sts on to st holder, rib to end, inc 6 (9, 8) sts evenly across row. 40 (43, 46) sts.
Change to larger needles and cont as for Back to armholes, ending with a p row.

Shape armhole and front edge
Next row: Cast/bind off 3 sts, k to last 2 sts, k2 tog.
Next row: P to end.
At front edge dec one st on every 3rd row until 12 (13, 14) sts in all have been dec at this edge, and AT THE SAME TIME at armhole edge dec one st at beg of next and every other row until 2 sts rem, ending with a p row. Cast/bind off.

RIGHT FRONT
With smaller needles and M, cast on 46 (46, 50) sts.
For man's version: Work 13 rows in rib as for Back.
For woman's version: Work 6 rows in rib as for Back.
7th row: Rib 5, cast/bind off 2 sts, rib to end.
8th row: Rib to end, casting on 2 sts over those cast/bound off.
Work 5 more rows in rib.

For both versions:
14th row: Rib 34 (34, 38) sts, inc 6 (9, 8) sts evenly across these sts, then turn and leave rem 12 sts on st holder. 40 (43, 46) sts.
Change to larger needles and cont to match Left Front, reversing all shaping.

SLEEVES
With smaller needles and M, cast on 42 (46, 50) sts and work 14 rows in rib as for Back, inc 7 (9, 11) sts evenly across last row. 49 (55, 61) sts.
Change to larger needles and beg with a k row, work in st st for 4 cm/1½″, ending with a p row.
Cont in st st, work 24 rows of patt from chart, then cont in M, and AT THE SAME TIME inc one st at each end of next and every foll 8th row until there are 61 (67, 73) sts.
Cont in M until sleeve measures 38 (39, 40) cm/15 (15¼, 15¾)″ from beg, then work the 1st–14th rows of patt from chart.

Shape top/cap
Working patt exactly as for Back armholes, cast/bind off 3 sts at beg of next 2 rows, then dec one st at each end of next and every other row until 9 (11, 13) sts rem, ending with a p row. Cast/bind off.

BUTTON BAND
Join raglan sleeves.
Sl 12 sts on to smaller needle and cont in rib until band, when slightly stretched, reaches to centre back neck. Cast/bind off in rib.
Pin band in place and mark positions of buttons with pins – first pin on 7th row from beg, 2nd pin just below beg of front shaping, then 2 more at equal intervals between these 2.

BUTTONHOLE BAND
Work to match button band, making buttonholes as before to correspond with positions of pins.

ASSEMBLY
Press work according to instructions on yarn band.
Join side and sleeve seams.
Sew on front bands, joining at centre back neck.
Press seams.
Sew on buttons.

Victorian Shawl

MATERIALS
8 20 g/1 oz balls (each approx 75 m/82 yds) of Lister–Lee *Tamarisk DK* (light weight mohair)
1 pair of 4 mm/No 6 knitting needles
4 mm/No 6 circular knitting needle
Crochet hook for fringe

MEASUREMENTS
Across top 155 cm/61″
Depth (excluding fringe) 61 cm/24″

INSTRUCTIONS
Using 4 mm/No 6 needles cast on 5 sts.
1st row: P1, k3, p1.
2nd row: K1, p3, k1.
3rd row: P1, yon/yo, sl 2 tog–k1–p2sso, yrn/yo, p1.
4th row: Cast on 4 sts, working across these sts, k1, p3, then k1, p3, k1.
5th row: Cast on 4 sts, working across these sts, p1, k3, then *p1, k3, rep from * to last st, p1.
6th row: K1, *p3, k1, rep from * to end.
7th row: P1, *yon/yo, sl 2 tog–k1–p2sso, yrn/yo, p1, rep from * to end.
8th row: Cast on 4 sts, k1, *p3, k1, rep from * to end.
Rep 5th–8th rows until there are 333 sts (changing to circular needle when necessary), ending with a 6th row. Cast/bind off.

ASSEMBLY
Do not press.
Cut yarn into lengths of approx 20 cm/8″ and using 4 strands tog each time, knot along shaped edges of shawl. Trim fringe.

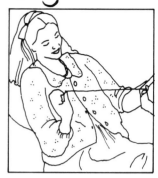

Bedjacket

MATERIALS
10 25 g/1 oz balls (each approx 85 m/95 yds) of Pingouin *Mohair/Mohair 50* (medium weight mohair)
1 pair each of 5 mm/No 8 and 6 mm/No 10 knitting needles
6 buttons
Ribbon for waist (optional)

MEASUREMENTS
To fit 86–97 cm/34–38″ bust
Length 55 cm/21¾″
Sleeve seam 42 cm/16½″

TENSION/GAUGE
14 sts and 16 rows to 10 cm/4″ over patt using 6 mm/No 10 needles.

BACK
With smaller needles, cast on 71 sts and work 14 rows in k1, p1 rib (beg first row k1).
Next row: Rib 3, *yfwd/yo, k2 tog, rib 6, rep from * to last 4 sts, yfwd/yo, k2 tog, rib 2.
Work 1 more row in rib, inc one st in centre of row. 72 sts.
Change to larger needles and cont in patt as foll:
1st row: K1, *k2 tog, yfwd/yo, k1, yfwd/yo, sl 1–k1–psso, k5, rep from * to last st, k1.
2nd row: P1, *p7, sl 1 purlwise, p2, rep from * to last st, p1.
3rd and 4th rows: As 1st and 2nd rows.
5th row: K to end.
6th row: P to end.
7th row: K1, *k5, k2 tog, yfwd/yo, k1, yfwd/yo, sl 1–k1–psso, rep from * to last st, k1.
8th row: P1, *p2, sl 1 purlwise, p7, rep from * to last st, p1.
9th and 10th rows: As 7th and 8th rows.
11th and 12th rows: As 5th

and 6th rows.
Rep these 12 rows for patt until work measures 36 cm/14¼'' from beg, ending with a WS row.

Shape armholes
Keeping to correct patt, cast/bind off 5 sts at beg of next 2 rows, 2 sts at beg of next 2 rows, then dec one st at each end of next and foll alt row. 54 sts.
Cont without shaping until armholes measure 17 cm/6¾'', ending with a WS row.

Shape neck
Next row: Patt 19, cast/bind off 16 sts, patt to end.
Cont on last 19 sts, dec one st at neck edge on next 2 rows, then cont without shaping until armhole measures 19 cm/7½'', ending with a WS row.
Cast/bind off.
Return to other 19 sts and work to match.

RIGHT FRONT
With smaller needles cast on 49 sts and work 6 rows in k1, p1 rib (beg first row k1).
Next row: (buttonhole row) Rib 4, yrn/yo, p2 tog, rib to end.
Work 7 more rows in rib.
Next row: Rib 8 and sl on to st holder, rib 3, *yfwd/yo, k2 tog, rib 6, rep from * to last 6 sts, yfwd/yo, k2 tog, rib 4.
Work 1 more row in rib, inc one st at beg of row. 42 sts.
Change to larger needles and cont in patt as for Back until work measures same as Back to armholes, ending with a RS row.

Shape armhole
Cast/bind off 5 sts at beg of next row, then 2 sts at beg of foll alt row. Dec one st at armhole edge on next and foll alt row. 33 sts.
Cont without shaping until armhole measures 10 cm/4'', ending with a WS row.

Shape neck
Cast/bind off 7 sts at beg of next row, 5 sts at beg of foll alt rows, then dec one st at neck edge on every row until 17 sts rem.
Cont without shaping until armhole measures as for Back, ending with a WS row.
Cast/bind off.

LEFT FRONT
Work to match Right Front,

omitting buttonhole and reversing all shaping.

SLEEVES
With smaller needles, cast on 35 sts and work in k1, p1 rib for 5 cm/2'', ending with a WS row and inc 7 sts evenly across last row. 42 sts.
Change to larger needles and cont in patt as for Back, inc one st at each end of every 8th row until there are 52 sts, then cont without shaping until sleeve measures 42 cm/16½'' from beg, ending with a WS row.

Shape top/cap
Cast/bind off 5 sts at beg of next 2 rows, then dec one st at each end of next and every other row until 18 sts rem, ending with a WS row.
Cast/bind off 4 sts at beg of next 2 rows, then cast/bind off rem 10 sts.

LEFT FRONT BAND
Sl 8 sts from st holder on to smaller needles and cont in rib until band, when slightly stretched, reaches to neck edge.
Cast/bind off.
Mark position of buttons on front band, the first on 7th row from beg, the 2nd about 2 cm/3¼'' below neck edge, then 4 more at equal intervals between these 2.

RIGHT FRONT BAND
Work to match Left Front Band, making buttonholes as before (see Right Front) to correspond with positions marked.

COLLAR
With larger needles cast on 62 sts and k 2 rows.
Work 16 rows in patt as for Back, inc one st at each end of next and every foll 4th row. 70 sts.
Next row: Cast on 16 sts, k these 16 sts, k twice into every st on needle, then turn and cast on 16 sts. 172 sts.
K 2 rows.
Cast/bind off.

ASSEMBLY
Join shoulder seams. Sew in sleeves.
Join side and sleeve seams.
Sew on front bands.
Stitch two sets of 16 sts to side edges of collar. Sew cast on edge on collar to neck edge, starting and ending

inside front bands.
Sew on buttons.
Thread ribbon through eyelet holes at waist if required.

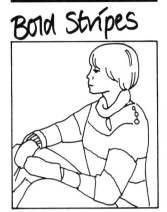

Bold Stripes

MATERIALS
3 (4) 40 g/1½ oz balls (each approx 132 m/144 yds) of Sirdar *Wash 'n' Wear Double Crepe* (double knitting / knitting worsted weight yarn) in 1st colour (A)
3 balls in 2nd colour (B)
2 balls in 3rd colour (C)
1 pair of 4½ mm/No 7 knitting needles
4½ mm/No 7 circular knitting needle
3.50 mm/size E crochet hook
4 buttons

MEASUREMENTS
To fit 84–89 (89–94) cm/33–35 (35–37)'' bust
Length 68 cm/26¾''
Sleeve seam 43 cm/17''

TENSION/GAUGE
20 sts and 36 rows to 10 cm/4'' over g st using 4½ mm/No 7 needles.

BACK
With 4½ mm/No 7 needles and A, cast on 97 (101) sts.
1st row: K2, *p1, k1, rep from * to last st, k1.
2nd row: *K1, p1, rep from * to last st, k1.
Rep these 2 rows 19 times more.
Break off A and join in B and work 36 rows in g st.
Break off B and join in C and work in moss/seed st as foll:
1st row: *K1, p1, rep from * to last st, k1.
Rep last row 31 times more.
Break off C and join in A and work 36 rows in g st.
Break off A and join in B and work 1 row in moss/seed st.

Shape armholes
Cont in moss/seed st, dec one

st at each end of next 3 (7) rows, then foll 14 (12) alt rows. Work 1 row.**

Break off yarn and leave rem 63 sts on spare needle.

FRONT
Work as for Back.

SLEEVES
With 4½ mm/No 7 needles and A, cast on 41 (43) sts.
Work 26 rows in rib as for Back.
Break off A and join in B.
Next row: K2 (3), inc one st, *k3, inc one st, rep from * to last 2 (3) sts, k to end. 51 (53) sts.
Work 35 rows in g st, and AT THE SAME TIME inc one st at each end of 6th and then every foll 8th row until there are 59 (61) sts.
Break off B and join in C.
Next row: K.
Work 33 rows in moss/seed st, and AT THE SAME TIME inc one st at each end of 2nd and every foll 8th row until there are 67 (69) sts.
Break off C and join in A.
Work 36 rows in g st, and AT THE SAME TIME inc one st at each end of next and every foll 8th row 3 (4) times. 75 (79) sts.
Break off A and join in B.
Next row: K.
Work 1 row in moss/seed st.

Shape top/cap
Cont in moss/seed st, work as for armholes on Back to **.
Break off yarn and leave rem 41 sts on spare needle.

YOKE
Press pieces lightly foll instructions on yarn band.
Set in sleeves.
Mark centre st on right sleeve top.
With RS of work facing, circular needle and A, beg with marked st, k to last st of sleeve top, k last st tog with first st of back, k to last st of back, k last st tog with first st of left sleeve, k to last st of sleeve, k last st tog with first st of front, k to last st on front, k last st tog with first st of sleeve, k sts of sleeve, ending again in centre st. Turn. 205 sts.
1st row: *K1, p1, rep from * to last st, k1.
2nd row: K2, *p1, k1, rep from * to last st, k1.

Rep last 2 rows twice more and 1st row again.
8th row: *Rib 9, sl 1–k2 tog–psso, rep from * to last st, k1. 171 sts.
Work 7 rows in rib.
16th row: *Rib 7, sl 1–k2 tog–psso, rep from * to last st, k1. 137 sts.
Work 7 rows in rib.
24th row: *Rib 5, sl 1–k2 tog–psso, rep from * to last st, k1. 103 sts.
Work 7 rows in rib.
32nd row: *Rib 3, sl 1–k2 tog–psso, rep from * to last st, k1. 69 sts.
Work 6 rows in rib.
Cast/bind off in rib.

ASSEMBLY
Join side and sleeve seams.
Using crochet hook and A, work a row of firm dc/sc along shoulder opening at front edge. Turn with 1ch and work another row of dc/sc, making 4 button loops equally spaced by working 2ch and missing/skipping 1dc/sc. Fasten off.
Press seams lightly.
Sew on buttons.

Rust Cardigan

MATERIALS
13 (14, 15, 17) 50 g/1¾ oz balls (each approx 120 m/131 yds) of Patons *Clansman DK* (double knitting/sport to knitting worsted weight yarn)
1 pair each of 3¼ mm/No 3 and 4 mm/No 6 knitting needles
3.50 mm/size E crochet hook
8 buttons

MEASUREMENTS
To fit 86 (91, 97, 102) cm/34 (36, 38, 40)″ bust

Length approx 55 (56, 57, 58) cm/21¾ (22, 22½, 22¾)″
Sleeve seam approx 44 cm/ 17¼″

TENSION/GAUGE
22 sts and 30 rows to 10 cm/ 4″ over moss/seed st patt using 4 mm/No 6 needles.

ABBREVIATIONS
MB = make bobble – [k1, yfwd/yo, k1, yfwd/yo, k1] all into next st, turn, k5, turn, p5, pass 2nd, 3rd, 4th and 5th sts over first st.
m st – moss/seed st.

BACK
With smaller needles, cast on 93 (99, 105, 111) sts.
1st row: K1, *p1, k1, rep from * to end.
2nd row: P1, *k1, p1, rep from * to end.
Rep these 2 rows for 6 cm/ 2½″, ending with a 2nd row.
Change to larger needles and cont in moss/seed st as foll:
Next row: K1, *p1, k1, rep from * to end.
Rep this row until work measures 32 cm/12½″ from beg, ending with a WS row.
Adjust length here if required, then cont in bobble patt:
1st row: M st 4, *MB, m st 5, rep from * to last 5 sts, MB, m st 4.
Work 5 rows in m st.
7th row: K1, *MB, m st 5, rep from * to last 2 sts, MB, k1.
Work 5 rows in m st.
These 12 rows form bobble patt.

Shape armholes
Keeping patt correct throughout, cast/bind off 2 sts at beg of next 4 rows, then dec one st at each end of next and foll 2 (3, 4, 5) alt rows. 79 (83, 87, 91) sts.
Cont without shaping until armholes measure 19 (20, 21, 22) cm/7½ (7¾, 8¼, 8¾)″, ending with a WS row.

Shape shoulders and neck
Cast/bind off 5 (6, 6, 7) sts at beg of next 4 rows.
Next row: Cast/bind off 5 (6, 6, 7) sts, patt 11 (10, 11, 10) including st on needle, turn.
Next row: Cast/bind off 5 sts, patt to end.
Cast/bind off rem 6 (5, 6, 5) sts.
Return to rem sts, rejoin yarn and cast/bind off 27 (27,

29, 29) sts, patt to end.
Cont to match first side.

LEFT FRONT
With smaller needles, cast on 47 (49, 53, 55) sts and work in rib as for Back for 6 cm/ 2½″, ending with a 2nd row and inc one st at end of last row on 2nd and 4th sizes. 47 (50, 53, 56) sts.
Change to larger needles and cont in m st until work measures same as Back to beg of bobble patt, ending with a WS row. (**Note:** On 2nd and 4th sizes odd numbered rows will end with p1 and even rows will beg with p1).
Cont in bobble patt as foll:
1st row: M st 4, *MB, m st 5, rep from * to last 7 (4, 7, 4) sts, MB, m st 6 (3, 6, 3).
Work 5 rows in m st.
7th row: K1, *MB, m st 5, rep from * to last 4 (7, 4, 7) sts, MB, m st 3 (6, 3, 6). Work 5 rows in m st.

Shape armhole and front edge
Keeping bobble patt correct, cast/bind off 2 sts at beg of next and foll alt row, then dec one st at beg of foll 3 (4, 5, 6) alt rows, but AT THE SAME TIME dec one st at front edge on 1st and every foll 3rd row until 21 (23, 24, 26) sts rem.
Cont without shaping until armhole measures as for Back, ending with a WS row.

Shape shoulder
Cast/bind off 5 (6, 6, 7) sts at beg of next and foll 2 alt rows. Work 1 row, then cast/bind off rem 6 (5, 6, 5) sts.

RIGHT FRONT
Work to match Left Front, reversing patt and all shaping.

SLEEVES
With smaller needles, cast on 45 (47, 49, 51) sts and work in rib as for Back for 6 cm/ 2½″, ending with a 2nd row and inc 10 sts evenly across last row. 55 (57, 59, 61) sts.
Change to larger needles and cont in moss/seed st as for Back, inc one st at each end of 1st and every foll 6th row until there are 79 (83, 87, 91) sts, then cont without shaping until sleeve measures 40 cm/14¾″ from beg, ending with a WS row.
Cont in bobble patt as foll:

1st row: M st 3 (2, 4, 3), *MB, m st 5, rep from * to last 4 (3, 5, 4) sts, MB, m st to end.
Work 5 rows in m st.
7th row: M st 6 (5, 7, 6), *MB, m st 5, rep from * to last 1 (0, 2, 1) sts, m st 1 (0, 2, 1).
Work 5 rows in m st.

Shape top/cap
Keeping patt correct, cast/bind off 2 sts at beg of next 4 rows.
Dec one st at each end of next and every other row until 27 sts rem, ending with a WS row.
Cast/bind off 2 sts at beg of next 6 rows.
Cast/bind off rem 15 sts.

FRONT EDGING
Join shoulder seams.
Mark positions of buttonholes on Right Front, the first 1 cm/½″ from lower edge, the 2nd just below beg of front shaping, then 6 more at equal intervals between these 2.
With crochet hook and RS facing, work 1 row of dc/sc up Right Front, across back neck and down Left Front, turn.
Work a 2nd row of dc/sc, working buttonholes at marked positions as foll: 2ch, miss/skip 2dc/sc, 1dc/sc into each dc/sc to next buttonhole.
Next row: 1ch, *1dc/sc into each of next 4 sts, 3ch, ss/sl st into last dc/sc, rep from * to end.
Fasten off.

ASSEMBLY
Press work, if necessary, according to instructions on yarn band.
Sew in sleeves, gathering top to fit.
Join side and sleeve seams.
Press seams.
Sew on buttons.

Yellow Leaves

MATERIALS
15 (17) 50 g/1¾ oz balls (each approx 80 m/90 yds) of Pingouin *Coton Naturel 8 fils* (medium weight cotton)
1 pair each of 3 mm/No 3 and 3¾ mm/No 5 knitting needles
3¾ mm/No 5 circular knitting needle
Set of four 3 mm/No 3 double-pointed knitting needles

MEASUREMENTS
To fit 76–81 (86–91) cm/30–32 (34–36)″ bust
Length 60 cm/23½″
Sleeve seam 46 cm/18″

TENSION/GAUGE
22 sts and 30 rows to 10 cm/4″ over moss/seed st patt on 3¾ mm/No 5 needles.

BACK
With smaller needles, cast on 91 (97) sts.
1st row: K2, *p3, k3, rep from * to last 5 sts, p3, k2.
2nd row: P2, *k3, p3, rep from * to last 5 sts, k3, p2.
Rep these 2 rows for 7 cm/2¾″, ending with a 2nd row and inc 4 (6) sts evenly across last row. 95 (103) sts.
Change to larger needles and cont in patt as foll:
1st row: K1, *p1, k1, rep from * to end.
2nd row: P1, *k1, p1, rep from * to end.
3rd row: As 2nd row.
4th row: As 1st row.
Rep these 4 rows until work measures 36 cm/14½″ from beg, ending with a WS row.
Cast/bind off 4 (5) sts at beg of next 2 rows.
Leave rem 87 (93) sts on spare needle.

FRONT
Work as for Back.

SLEEVES
With smaller needles, cast on 37 (43) sts and work in rib as for Back for 5 cm/2″, ending with a 1st row and inc one st at each end of last row. 39 (45) sts.
Next row: Rib 2 (4), *inc in next st, rib 4 (3), rep from * to last 2 (5) sts, inc in next st, rib 1 (4). 47 (55) sts.
Change to larger needles and cont in patt as for Back, inc one st at each end of 7th and every foll 8th row until there are 69 (77) sts, then cont without shaping until sleeve measures 46 cm/18″ from beg, ending with a WS row.
Cast/bind off 4 (5) sts at beg of next 2 rows. Leave rem 61 (67) sts on spare needle.

YOKE
With circular needle and RS facing, k across sts of back, left sleeve, front and right sleeve, knitting 2 tog at each seam, and also inc one st at Centre Back and Centre Front on 1st size, dec one st at Centre Back on 2nd size. 294 (315) sts.
Then k43 (46) to Centre Back and beg rounds from here.
1st round: Yfwd/yo, *k1, yrn/yo, p6, yon/yo, rep from * to last 7 sts, k1, yrn/yo, p6.
2nd and every alt round: K to end.
3rd round: *K1, [yfwd/yo, k1] twice, p6, rep from * to end.
5th round: *K2, yfwd/yo, k1, yfwd/yo, k2, p6, rep from * to end.
7th round: *K2, inc 1 by knitting twice into next st, k1, inc 1, k2, p6, rep from * to end.
9th round: *Sl 1–k1–psso, k5, k2 tog, p6, rep from * to end.
11th round: *Sl 1–k1–psso, k3, k2 tog, p6, rep from * to end.
13th round: *Sl 1–k1–psso, k1, k2 tog, p6, rep from * to end.
15th round: *Sl 1–k2 tog–psso, p6, rep from * to end.
17th round: P to end.
18th round: K to end.
19th round: *P1, p2 tog, rep from * to end. 196 (210) sts.
20th round: K to end.
21st–38th rounds: Rep 1st–

18th rounds.

39th round: *P0 (1), [p2 tog, p1] 4 (2) times, p2 tog, p0 (1), rep from * to end. 126 (147) sts.

40th round: K to end.

41st–58th rounds: Rep 1st–18th rounds.

59th round: *P1, p2 tog, rep from * to end. 84 (98) sts.

60th round: On 1st size, k to end, on 2nd size [k2 tog, k47] twice. 84 (96) sts.

Change to set of four double-pointed needles and work in rounds of k3, p3 rib for 2.5 cm/1″.

Cast/bind off in rib.

ASSEMBLY

Join side, sleeve and under-arm seams. Press, if necessary, as instructed on yarn band.

MATERIALS

6 (7, 7) 25 g/1 oz balls (each approx 49 m/54 yds) of Lister-Lee *Tahiti* (medium weight mohair) in main colour (M)

2 balls in contrast colour (C)

Small amount of black yarn (D)

1 pair each of 4 mm/No 6 and 5 mm/No 8 knitting needles

6 buttons

MEASUREMENTS

To fit approx 4 (6, 8) years

Chest 61 (66, 71) cm/24 (26, 28)″

Length 39 (43, 48) cm/15½ (17, 18¾)″

Sleeve seam 27 (32, 37) cm/ 10¾ (12½, 14½)″

TENSION/GAUGE

16 sts and 22 rows to 10 cm/ 4″ over st st using 5 mm/No 8 needles.

BACK

With smaller needles and C, cast on 51 (55, 59) sts and work in k1, p1 rib for 5 cm/2″, ending with a WS row.

Break off C.

Change to larger needles, join in M and cont in st st until work measures 27 (29, 32) cm/10¾ (11½, 12½)″, ending with a p row.

Shape armholes

Cast/bind off 2 sts at beg of next 2 rows, then dec one st at each end of next 4 rows. 39 (43, 47) sts.

Cont without shaping until armholes measure 12 (14, 16) cm/4¾ (5½, 6¼)″, ending with a p row.

Shape shoulders

Cast/bind off 6 (6, 7) sts at beg of next 2 rows, then 6 (7, 7) sts at beg of next 2 rows.

Cast/bind off rem 15 (17, 19) sts.

LEFT FRONT

With smaller needles and C, cast on 25 (27, 29) sts and work in k1, p1 rib for 5 cm/2″, ending with a WS row.

Break off C.

Change to larger needles, join in M and cont in st st until work measures as for Back to armholes, ending with a p row.

Shape armhole

Cast/bind off 2 sts at beg of next row, then work 1 row.

Dec one st at armhole edge on next 4 rows. 19 (21, 23) sts.

Cont without shaping until armhole is 7 rows less than Back to shoulders, ending with a k row.

Shape neck

Cast/bind off 2 (3, 4) sts at beg of next row, then dec one st at neck edge on next 5 rows.

Work 1 row.

Shape shoulders

Cast/bind off 6 (6, 7) sts at beg of next row.

Work 1 row, then cast/bind off rem 6 (6, 7) sts.

RIGHT FRONT

Work to match Left Front, reversing all shaping.

SLEEVES

With smaller needles and C, cast on 25 (27, 29) sts and work in k1, p1 rib for 5 cm/2″, ending with a WS row.

Break off C.

Change to larger needles, join in M and cont in st st, inc one st at each end of 3rd and every foll 6th row until there are 39 (43, 47) sts, then cont without shaping until sleeve measures 27 (32, 37) cm/10¾ (12½, 14½)″, ending with a p row.

Shape top/cap

Cast/bind off 2 sts at beg of next 2 rows.

Dec one st at each end of next and every other row until 17 sts rem, ending with a p row.

Cast/bind off 2 sts at beg of next 4 rows, then cast/bind off rem 9 sts.

BUTTON BAND

With smaller needles and C, cast on 7 sts and work in k1, p1 rib until band, when slightly stretched, reaches to neck edge, ending with a WS row.

Cast/bind off.

Mark position of buttons on band, the first 2.5 cm/1″ from lower edge, the 2nd 4 rows from top edge, then 4 more at equal intervals between these 2.

BUTTONHOLE BAND

Work to match Button Band, making buttonholes as foll (with RS facing):

Buttonhole row: K1, p1, k1, yfwd/yo, k2 tog, p1, k1.

COLLAR

With smaller needles and C, cast on 58 (64, 70) sts.

1st row: K1, *p2, k1, rep from * to end.

2nd row: P1, *k2, p1, rep from * to end.

Rep these 2 rows 6 (7, 8) times more.

Next row: K1, *p2 tog, k1, rep from * to end.

Next row: P1, *k1, p1, rep from * to end.

Cast/bind off in rib.

ASSEMBLY

Embroider motifs in Swiss darning/duplicate st on fronts, the first 2.5 (5.5) cm/1 (2¼)″ from top of ribbing, the second 2.5 cm/1″ below neck shaping, then the third halfway between these 2. Each motif should beg on 3rd (4th, 5th) st from front edge.

Join shoulder seams.

Sew in sleeves.

Join side and sleeve seams.

Sew on front bands.

Sew cast/bound-off edge of collar to neck edge, beg and ending in centre of front bands.

Sew on buttons.

HAT

With smaller needles and C,

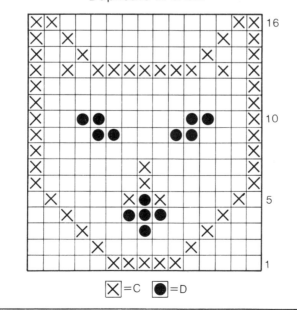

Swiss darning
Duplicate st chart

☒ = C   ⬤ = D

Pussycat motif is applied with Swiss darning/duplicate stitch.

cast on 57 (61, 65) sts and k 4 rows.
Change to larger needles and cont in st st until work measures 20 cm/7¾" from beg, or length required, ending with a p row.

Shape top
1st row: *K2, k2 tog, rep from * to last st, k1.
2nd row: P to end.
3rd row: *K1, k2 tog, rep from * to last st, k1.
4th row: P1, *p2 tog, rep from * to end.
Break off yarn, thread through sts, gather up and fasten off.
Join back seam.

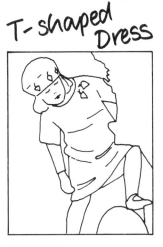

T-shaped Dress

MATERIALS
4 (4, 5, 6) 50 g/1¾ oz balls (each approx 168 m/184 yds) of Sirdar *Country Style DK* (double knitting/sport to knitting worsted weight yarn) in main colour (M)
Small amounts in 3 contrasting colours for motifs (A, B and C)
1 pair each of 3¾ mm/No 5 and 3¼ mm/No 3 knitting needles

MEASUREMENTS
To fit approx 3 (4, 5, 6) years
Length 48 (53, 57, 61) cm/ 20½ (20¾, 22½, 24)"

TENSION/GAUGE
24 sts and 32 rows to 10 cm/ 4" over st st using 3¾ mm/ No 5 needles.
Note: The dress is knitted in one piece, beg at lower edge of front and ending at lower edge of back.

INSTRUCTIONS
With larger needles and M, cast on 91 (93, 97, 101) sts.

Beg with a k row, work 8 rows in st st.
Next row: (picot row) K1 (0, 1, 2), *k1, yfwd/yo, k2 tog, rep from * to end.
Beg with a p row, cont in st st, dec one st at each end of every 7th row 15 times. 61 (63, 67, 71) sts.
Mark last row with a coloured thread.
Cont in st st without shaping until work measures 34 (37, 39, 42) cm/13½ (14½, 15¼, 16½)" from picot hemline, ending with a k row (note how many rows have been worked straight from coloured thread).
Change to smaller needles and work in g st for bodice.
Cont in g st without shaping for 2.5 (4, 4, 4) cm/1 (1½, 1½, 1½)" ending with a WS row.
Cont in g st, cast on 19 (21, 23, 25) sts at beg of next 2 rows for sleeves.
Cont on all 99 (105, 113, 121) sts until work measures 44 (48, 52, 55) cm/17¼ (19, 20½, 21¾)" from hemline, ending with a RS row.
Next row: K35 (37, 40, 43) sts and leave on spare needle, cast/bind off next 29 (31, 33, 35) sts for neck, k to end.
K 21 (25, 25, 29) rows on these last 35 (37, 40, 43) sts. Cast on 29 (31, 33, 35) sts for neck. Break off yarn and place sts on a st holder.
Rejoin yarn to first set of 35 (37, 40, 43) sts at neck edge and k 22 (26, 26, 30) rows.
Next row: K35 (37, 40, 43), k across 29 (31, 33, 35) sts at back neck, then k across rem 35 (37, 40, 43) sts on st holder. 99 (105, 113, 121) sts.
Cont in g st on all sts until back measures same as front from shoulder line to end of sleeve sts, ending with a WS row.
Cast/bind off 19 (21, 23, 25) sts at beg of next 2 rows. 61 (63, 67, 71) sts.
Cont in g st without shaping for 2.5 (4, 4, 4) cm/1 (1½, 1½, 1½)", ending with a WS row.
Change to larger needles and beg with a k row, work in st st without shaping until same number of rows have been worked as on straight part of front.
Inc one st at each end of next row and every foll 7th row until there are 91 (93, 97, 101) sts.
Cont in st st without shaping

until work measures same as front to picot row, ending with a p row.
Next row: (picot row) K1 (0, 1, 2), *k1, yfwd/yo, k2 tog, rep from * to end.
Beg with a p row, work 7 rows in st st. Cast/bind off.

ASSEMBLY
Foll chart for matching baby's dress, work 2 cross st raspberries near Left Front neck edge.
Press lightly foll instructions on yarn band.
Join side and underarm seams.
Fold hem along picot row and sew in place.

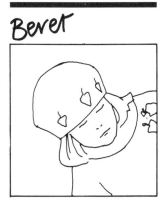

Beret

MATERIALS
1 50 g/1¾ oz ball (each approx 168 m/184 yds) of Sirdar *Country Style DK* (double knitting/sport to knitting worsted weight yarn) in main colour (M)
Small amounts in 3 contrasting colours for motifs (A, B and C)
1 pair of 4 mm/No 6 knitting needles

MEASUREMENTS
To fit small child's head

TENSION/GAUGE
24 sts and 40 rows to 10 cm/ 4" over garter st.

INSTRUCTIONS
With M, cast on 70 sts.
K 4 rows.
5th row: *K9, inc in next st, rep from * to end.
6th and every foll alt row: K.
7th row: *K10, inc in next st, rep from * to end.
9th row: *K11, inc in next st, rep from * to end.
11th row: *K12, inc in next st, rep from * to end.
13th row: *K13, inc in next st, rep from * to end.

15th row: *K14, inc in next st, rep from * to end.
17th row: *K15, inc in next st, rep from * to end.
K 15 rows without shaping.
33rd row: *K15, k2 tog, rep from * to end.
34th and every foll alt row: K.
35th row: *K14, k2 tog, rep from * to end.
37th row: *K13, k2 tog, rep from * to end.
39th row: *K12, k2 tog, rep from * to end.
Cont to dec in this way, working one st less on every alt row until the row *k1, k2 tog, rep from * to end has been completed.
Next row: *K2 tog, rep from * to end.
Break off yarn, leaving a long end and thread through rem sts, gather and fasten off.

ASSEMBLY
Sew up seam.
Foll chart for matching baby's dress, work cross st raspberries on front of beret.

Baby's Smock

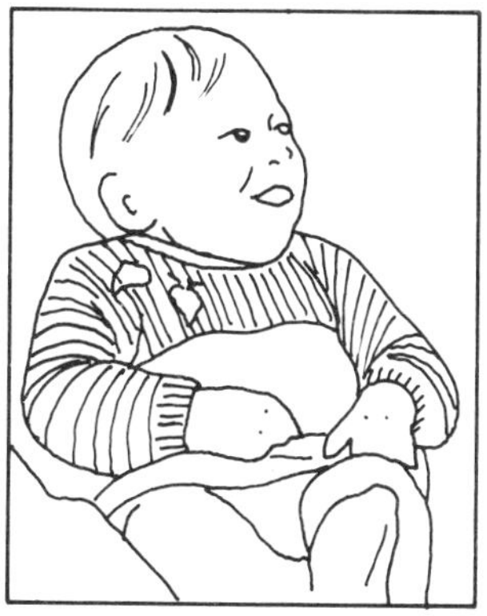

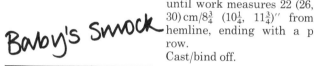

MATERIALS
4 (4, 5) 50 g/$1\frac{3}{4}$ oz balls (each approx. 238 m/260 yds) of Sirdar *Country Style 4-ply* (4 ply/sport weight yarn) in main colour (M)
Small amounts of 3 contrasting colours for motifs (A, B and C)
1 pair each of $3\frac{1}{4}$ mm/No 3 and $2\frac{3}{4}$ mm/No 2 knitting needles
3 buttons

MEASUREMENTS
To fit 46 (51, 56) cm/18 (20, 22)″ chest
Length 31 (36, 41) cm/$12\frac{1}{4}$ ($14\frac{1}{4}$, $16\frac{1}{4}$)″
Sleeve Seam 16 (19, 23) cm/$6\frac{1}{4}$ ($7\frac{1}{2}$, 9)″

TENSION/GAUGE
28 sts and 36 rows to 10 cm/4″ over st st using $3\frac{1}{4}$ mm/No 3 needles.

SKIRT (make 2 pieces)
Using smaller needles and M, cast on 84 (94, 104) sts.
Beg with a k row, work 7 rows in st st.
8th row: (WS) K, to mark hemline.
Change to larger needles and beg with a k row, work 18 rows in st st.
19th row: [K14 (16, 18), k2 tog] twice, k20 (22, 24), [sl 1–k1–psso, k14 (16, 18)] twice.
Beg with a p row, work 13 rows in st st.
33rd row: [K13 (15, 17), k2 tog] twice, k20 (22, 24), [sl 1–k1–psso, k13 (15, 17)] twice.
Cont to dec 4 sts in the same way every 14th row until 68 (74, 80) sts rem.
Cont in st st without shaping until work measures 22 (26, 30) cm/$8\frac{3}{4}$ ($10\frac{1}{4}$, $11\frac{3}{4}$)″ from hemline, ending with a p row.
Cast/bind off.

FRONT SLEEVES AND YOKE
Using smaller needles and M, cast on 19 (23, 25) sts for left cuff.
Work 8 rows in k1, p1 rib, inc one st at end of last row on 1st and 3rd sizes. 20 (23, 26) sts.
Change to larger needles and work in patt as foll:
1st row: K.
2nd and 3rd rows: P.
4th row: K.
Cont in patt until 60 (72, 88) patt rows have been worked, but inc one st at end of 49th row and mark this row.

Left shoulder
Work another 28 (32, 36) rows in patt, ending with a 4th patt row.

Shape front neck
1st row: Cast/bind off 4 sts, k to end.
2nd row: P until 4 sts rem, k4.
3rd row: K3, k2 tog, p to end.
4th row: K.
5th row: K3, k2 tog, k to end.

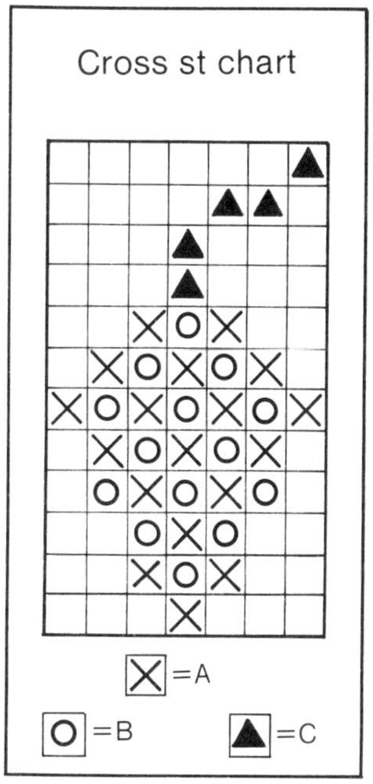

Cross stitch raspberries.

6th row: As 2nd row.
Keeping patt correct and 4 garter sts at neck edge, dec one st at neck edge in same way on next 2 (3, 4) RS rows. 13 (15, 17) sts.
Cont without shaping, keeping garter st border until 28 (30, 32) rows have been worked from beg of neck shaping.
Cont in patt as foll:
Next row: K4, make one st by lifting yarn between sts on row below and working tbl either knitwise or purlwise as patt requires, patt to end.
Next row: Patt until 4 sts rem, k4.
Rep these last 2 rows 3 (4, 5) times more.
Next row: K4, patt to end.
Next row: Patt to end, cast on 4 sts. 21 (24, 27) sts.

Right shoulder
Work 28 (32, 36) rows in patt on all sts and mark last row.

Right sleeve
Patt 12 (24, 40) rows. Patt 48 rows, dec one st at end of 1st row and at end of final row on 1st and 3rd sizes. 19 (23, 25) sts.

Cuff
Change to smaller needles and work 8 rows in k1, p1 rib.
Cast/bind off in rib.

BACK SLEEVES AND YOKE
Right sleeve and shoulder
Work as for left cuff, sleeve and shoulder for front, until beg of front neck shaping.
Then keeping garter st border at neck edge, work 16 (18, 20) rows without shaping.
K 6 rows for button band.
Cast/bind off.

Left side of back
Beg in centre of back, using larger needles and M, cast on 21 (24, 27) sts and k4 rows for buttonhole band.
Next row: (buttonhole row) K3, *yfwd/yo, k2 tog, k4 (5, 6), rep from * twice more.
Next row: K.
Beg with 3rd (1st, 3rd) row of 4 row patt and keeping 4 st garter st border at neck edge, work 16 (18, 20) rows.
Complete as for front right shoulder, right sleeve and cuff.

ASSEMBLY
Foll chart, work 2 cross st raspberries near Right Front neck edge.
Press st st parts lightly foll instructions on yarn band.
Join side seams of skirt.
Turn up hem at hemline and stitch down neatly to WS.
Join seams on top of sleeves and shoulders, then join underarm seams as far as marked points. Sew front yoke to front of skirt.
Catch button bands to overlap at back yoke then sew back yoke to back of skirt.
Press seams.
Sew on buttons.
Work overcast stitch around neck edge with A.

Cream Top

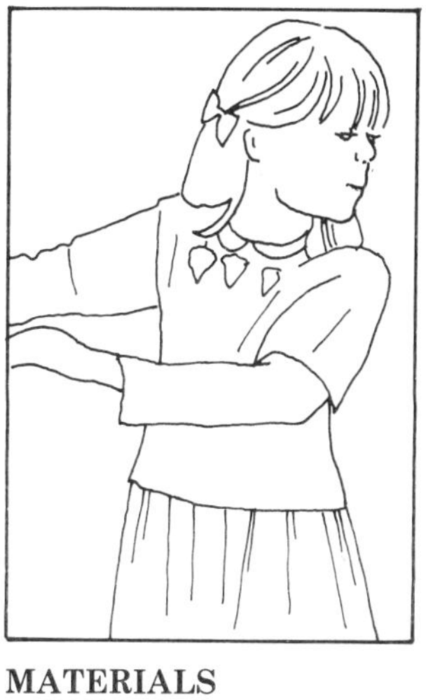

MATERIALS
3 (4, 4) 50 g/$1\frac{3}{4}$ oz balls (each

approx 168 m/184 yds) of Sirdar *Country Style DK* (double knitting/sport to knitting worsted weight yarn) in main colour (M)

Small amounts of 3 contrasting colours for motifs (A, B and C)

1 pair of 3¾ mm/No 5 knitting needles

MEASUREMENTS

To fit 56 (61, 66) cm/22 (24, 26)″ chest

Length 29 (34, 39) cm/11½ (13½, 15½)″

TENSION/GAUGE

22 sts and 36 rows to 10 cm/4″ over g st using 3¾ mm/No 5 needles.

Note: The sweater is worked in one piece from cuff to cuff.

INSTRUCTIONS

With M, cast on 50 (54, 58) sts.

Work 9 cm/3½″ in g st.

Cast on 39 (48, 57) sts at beg of next 2 rows for body. 128 (150, 172) sts.

Work without shaping on these sts for 9 (10, 11) cm/ 3½ (4, 4¼)″.

Shape neck

Next row: K57 (66, 75) sts and leave sts on spare needle, cast/bind off 14 (18, 22) sts, k to end.

Work without shaping on last set of 57 (66, 75) sts for 10 (11, 12) cm/4 (4¼, 4¾)″, ending at neck edge.

Leave these sts on spare needle, break yarn.

Rejoin yarn to rem set of 57 (66, 75) sts and work 10 (11, 12) cm/4 (4¼, 4¾)″ in g st, ending at neck edge.

Cast on 14 (18, 22) sts, k other set of 57 (66, 75) sts. 128 (150, 172) sts.

Work without shaping for 9 (10, 11) cm 3½ (4, 4¼)″.

Shape sleeves

Cast/bind off 39 (48, 57) sts at beg of next 2 rows. Cont without shaping on rem 50 (54, 58) sts for 9 cm/3½″.

Cast/bind off.

ASSEMBLY

Foll chart for matching baby's dress, work 3 cross st strawberries along front neck edge.

Join side and sleeve seams.

Country Cottage

MATERIALS

3 (4, 4, 5) 50 g/1¾ oz balls (each approx 142 m/155 yds) of Robin *Columbine Crepe DK* (double knitting/knitting worsted weight yarn) in main colour (M)

1 ball in each of 3 contrast colours (A, B and C)

Small amount in red for embroidery

1 pair each of 3¼ mm/No 3 and 4 mm/No 6 knitting needles

Set of four 3¼ mm/No 3 double-pointed knitting needles

MEASUREMENTS

To fit approx 2 (4, 6, 8) years

Chest 56 (61, 66, 71) cm/22 (24, 26, 28)″

Length 31 (35, 39, 43) cm/12¼ (13¾, 15¼, 17)″

Sleeve seam 26 (30, 34, 38) cm/ 10¼ (11¾, 13½, 15)″

TENSION/GAUGE

20 sts and 40 rows to 10 cm/4″ over g st using 4 mm/No 6 needles.

BACK

With smaller needles and A, cast on 63 (67, 73, 77) sts and work in k1, p1 rib for 5 cm/2″, ending with a WS row.

Break off A.

Change to larger needles, join in M and *cont in g st for 4 (6, 8, 10) cm/1½ (2½, 3¼, 4)″, ending with a WS row.

Break off M.

Join in C and k 1 row, then work 7 rows in moss/seed st.

Break off C, join in B, k 1 row, then work 15 rows in moss/seed st.

Break off B, join M.*

Rep from * to * once more, then cont in g st in M until

work measures 31 (35, 39, 43) cm/12¼ (13¾, 15¼, 17)″ from beg, ending with a WS row.

Next row: Cast/bind off 17 (18, 20, 21) sts, k until there are 29 (31, 33, 35) sts on RH needle, cast/bind off rem 17 (18, 20, 21) sts.

Leave centre sts on st holder.

FRONT

Work as for Back until work measures 27 (31, 35, 39) cm/ 10¾ (12¼, 13¾, 15¼)″, ending with a WS row.

Shape neck

Next row: K21 (22, 24, 25), turn and leave rem sts on spare needle.

Dec one st at neck edge on next 4 rows, then cont without shaping until work measures as for Back to shoulders, ending with a WS row.

Cast/bind off.

Return to sts on spare needle, sl first 21 (23, 25, 27) sts on to st holder for neck, rejoin yarn and k to end.

Cont to match first side.

SLEEVES

With smaller needles and A, cast on 29 (31, 33, 35) sts and work in k1, p1 rib for 5 cm/2″, ending with a RS row.

Next row: Inc in first st, *k1, inc in next st, rep from * to end. 44 (47, 50, 53) sts.

Break off A.

Change to larger needles, join in M and cont in g st, inc one st at each end of every 12th row until there are 50 (55, 60, 65) sts, then cont without shaping until sleeve measures 26 (30, 34, 38) cm/ 10¼ (11¾, 13½, 15)″, ending with a WS row.

Cast/bind off loosely.

NECKBAND

Join shoulder seams.

With set of four double-pointed needles and A, k back neck sts, inc 7 (7, 8, 8) sts across them, pick up and k12 sts down Left Front neck, k front neck sts, inc 5 (5, 6, 6) sts across them, then pick up and k12 sts up Right Front neck. 86 (90, 96, 100) sts.

Work 7 rounds in k1, p1 rib.

Cast/bind off in rib.

HOUSE

With larger needles and B, cast on 28 sts and work in g

st for 5 cm/2", ending with a WS row.
Break off B.
With C, cast on 4 sts, k28 sts on needle, turn and cast on 4 sts. 36 sts.
Cont in g st, dec at each end of 4th and every alt row until 20 sts rem.
Cast/bind off.

Doors and windows
With larger needles and C, cast on 6 sts and work in g st for 4 cm/1½".
Cast/bind off.
Make two more pieces in same way.

TREE
With larger needles and A, cast on 5 sts and work in g st for 4 cm/1½".
Cast on 4 sts at beg of next 2 rows, then inc one st at each end of next and foll alt row. 17 sts.
K3 rows.
Dec one st at beg of next row and at this same edge on next 2 rows. 14 sts.
Next row: K2 tog, k11, inc in last st.
Next row: Inc in first st, k11, k2 tog.
Next row: Inc in first st, k to end.
Next row: K to last st, inc in last st. 16 sts.
K 1 row.
Next row: K2 tog, k14.
Next row: K13, k2 tog.
Next row: K2 tog, [k4, k2 tog] twice.
Next row: K2 tog, k4, turn and cont on these sts only, dec one st at beg of next 3 rows, cast/bind off rem 2 sts.
Rejoin A to other 5 sts and k to end.
Dec one st at each end of next row, then cast/bind off rem 3 sts.

CLOUD
With B, cast on 4 sts and k1 row. Inc one st at each end of next 2 rows.
Next row: K8, turn and cast on 3 sts.
K 1 row.
Next row: K10, inc in last st.
Next row: Inc in first st, k11.
K 2 rows.
Next row: K2 tog, k11, turn and cast on 4 sts.
Next row: K14, k2 tog.
Next row: Inc in first st, k14.

Next row: K15, inc in last st.
Dec one st at end of next 3 rows.
Next row: Cast/bind off 2 sts, k10, k2 tog.
Cast/bind off 2 sts at beg of next row.
Dec one st at each end of next 2 rows.
Cast/bind off rem 5 sts.

ASSEMBLY
Do not press.
Sew in sleeves.
Join side and sleeve seams.
Sew door and windows to house as in picture, then sew house to front of sweater, leaving side open.
Sew on tree and cloud as in picture.
Embroider apples on tree in red.

Fairisle

MATERIALS
2 50 g/1¾ oz balls (each approx 125 m/137 yds) of Patons *Moorland Shetland DK* (double knitting/sport to knitting worsted weight yarn) in main colour (M)
1 ball in each of 4 contrast colours (A, B, C and D).
1 pair each of 3 mm/No 3 and 3¾ mm/No 5 knitting needles
Set of four 3 mm/No 3 double-pointed knitting needles

MEASUREMENTS
To fit approx 7–9 (9–11) years
Chest 70 (75) cm/27½ (29½)"
Length 44 (59) cm/17¼ (19½)"

TENSION/GAUGE
24 sts and 32 rows to 10 cm/4" over st st using 3¾ mm/No 5 needles

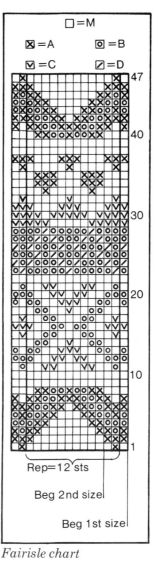

□ = M
⊠ = A   ⊙ = B
☑ = C   ◪ = D

Fairisle chart

Rep = 12 sts

Beg 2nd size

Beg 1st size

BACK
With smaller needles and M, cast on 85 (93) sts.
1st row: K1, *p1, k1, rep from * to end.
2nd row: P1, *k1, p1, rep from * to end.
Rep these 2 rows for 6 cm/2½", ending with a 2nd row and inc one st at each end of last row. 87 (95) sts.**
Change to larger needles and cont in st st until work measures 28 (32) cm/11 (12½)" from beg, ending with a p row.

Shape armholes
Cast/bind off 8 sts at beg of next 2 rows. 71 (79) sts.
Cont without shaping until armholes measure 16 (18) cm/6¼ (7)", ending with a p row.

Shape shoulders and neck
Cast/bind off 6 sts at beg of next 4 rows.
Next row: Cast/bind off 5 (6), k until there are 5 (6) sts on RH needle, turn.

Next row: P to end.
Cast/bind off 5 (6) sts. Sl next 27 (31) sts on to st holder for neck, rejoin yarn and k to end.
Cont to match first side.

FRONT
Work as for Back to **.
Change to larger needles and cont in st st until work measures 8 cm/3¼" from beg, ending with a p row.
Cont in st st, working in patt from chart, reading odd numbered rows from right to left and even rows from left to right.
Work in patt until band is completed, then cont in M only until work measures same as for Back to armholes, ending with a p row.

Shape armholes
Shape armholes as for Back, then cont without shaping until armholes measure 3 cm/1¼", ending with a p row.

Divide for neck
Next row: K35 (39), turn and leave rem sts on spare needle.
Dec one st at neck edge on every other row until 22 (24) sts rem, then cont without shaping until armhole measures as for Back, ending with a p row.

Shape shoulder
Cast/bind off 6 sts at beg of next and foll alt row, then 5 (6) sts at beg of foll alt row.
P 1 row, then cast/bind off rem 5 (6) sts.
Return to sts on spare needle, sl first st on to st holder for neck, rejoin yarn and k to end.
Cont to match first side.

NECKBAND
Join shoulder seams.
With set of four double-pointed needles, M and RS facing, pick up and k2 sts down right back neck, k back neck sts, pick up and k2 sts up Left Back neck and 40 (46) sts down Left Front neck, k Centre Front st from st holder, then pick up and k40 (46) sts up Right Front neck. 112 (128) sts.
Next round: Work in k1, p1 rib to 2 sts before Centre Front st, sl 1–k1–psso, k1, k2 tog, rib to end.
Rep this round for 3 cm/1¼".

Cast/bind off in rib, still dec at Centre Front.

ARMHOLE BORDERS
With smaller needles, M and RS facing, pick up and k75 (91) sts along straight edge of armhole.
Beg with a 2nd row, work in rib as for Back for 3 cm/1¼″.
Cast/bind off in rib.

ASSEMBLY
Press work according to instruction on yarn band.
Sew edges of armhole borders to cast/bound-off sts at armholes.
Join side seams.
Press seams.

Sun Dress

MATERIALS
5 (6, 7) 50 g/1¾ oz balls (each approx 200 m/220 yds) of Pingouin *Coton Perle* (light weight cotton)
1 pair each of 2¾ mm/No 2 and 3 mm/No 3 knitting needles
2 buttons

MEASUREMENTS
To fit approx 6 (8, 10) years
Chest approx 66 (71, 76) cm/ 26 (28, 30)″
Length 63 (68, 73) cm/24¾ (26¾, 28¾)″

TENSION/GAUGE
28 sts and 38 rows to 10 cm/4″ over patt using 3 mm/No 3 needles.

DRESS

FRONT
With smaller needles, cast on 151 (163, 175) sts and beg with a k row, work 8 rows in st st.
Next row: (picot row) K1,

*yfwd/yo, k2 tog, rep from * to end.
Change to larger needles and beg with a p row, work 9 rows in st st, then cont in patt as foll:
Beg with a k row, work 4 rows in st st.
5th row: K7 (13, 7), *yfwd/yo, k2 tog, k2, yfwd/yo, k2 tog, k18, rep from * to last 0 (6, 0) sts, k0 (6, 0).
Work 3 rows in st st.
9th row: K5 (11, 5), *[yfwd/yo, k2 tog, k2] twice, yfwd/yo, k2 tog, k14, rep from * to last 2 (8, 2) sts, k2 (8, 2) sts.
Work 3 rows in st st.
13th row: As 5th row.
Work 9 rows in st st.
23rd row: K19 (25, 19), *yfwd/yo, k2 tog, k2, yfwd/yo, k2 tog, k18, rep from * to last 12 (18, 12) sts, yfwd/yo, k2 tog, k2, yfwd/yo, k2 tog, k6 (12, 6).
Work 3 rows.
27th row: K17 (23, 17), *[yfwd/yo, k2 tog, k2] twice, yfwd/yo, k2 tog, k14, rep from * to last 14 (20, 14) sts, [yfwd/yo, k2 tog, k2] twice, yfwd/yo, k2 tog, k4 (10, 4).
Work 3 rows.
31st row: As 23rd row.
Work 5 rows.
These 36 rows form patt and are rep throughout.
Cont in patt, dec one st at each end of next row and every foll 36th row twice more. 145 (157, 169) sts.
For 1st size cont without shaping to 31st row of 4th patt; for 2nd size cont without shaping to end of 4th patt, then work 9 rows in st st; for 3rd size work without shaping to 13th row of 5th patt, then work 10 rows in st st, so ending with a RS row on all sizes.
Next row: P3, [p2 tog, p1] 47 (51, 55) times, p1. 98 (106, 114) sts.
Change to smaller needles and cont in rib as foll:
1st row: K2, *p2, k2, rep from * to end.
2nd row: P2, *k2, p2, rep from * to end.
Rep these 2 rows until work measures 50 (54, 58) cm/19¾ (21¼, 22¾)″ from hemline (picot row), ending with a WS row.
Cast/bind off loosely in rib.

BACK
Work as for Front until 4 rows less than Front, ending

with a WS row.
Next row: Rib 32 (35, 38), cast/bind off 2 sts, rib to last 34 (37, 40) sts, cast/bind off 2 sts, rib to end.
Next row: Rib to end, casting on 2 sts over each 2 cast/ bound off.
Work 2 more rows in rib, then cast/bind off in rib.

STRAPS (make 2)
With smaller needles, cast on 6 sts.
1st row: K2, p2, k2.
2nd row: K1, p1, k2, p1, k1.
Rep these 2 rows until work measures 26 (28, 30) cm/10¼ (11, 11¾)″, ending with a 2nd row.
Cast/bind off but do not break off yarn.
Using same needle and with RS facing, pick up and k75 (81, 87) sts along side of strap.
Beg with a p row, work 3 rows in st st.
Work picot row as at beg of Front, then beg with a p row, work 2 more rows in st st and cast/bind off.
Work in same way along other side of strap.

ASSEMBLY
Press work according to instructions on yarn band, omitting ribbing.
Join side seams.
Turn up hem at lower edge and sew in place.
Turn in edges of straps on picot row and sew in place.
Sew straps to top of front and sew a button to other end of each strap.
Press seams.

SOCKS
With smaller needles, cast on 49 (53, 57) sts and beg with a k row, work 6 rows in st st, then work picot row as for beg of Front.
Change to larger needles and cont in st st until work measures 7 cm/2¾″ from picot row, ending with a p row.
Break off yarn.

Divide for heel
Sl first and last 12 (13, 14) sts on to one needle with seam in centre, sl rem 25 (27, 29) sts on to a thread and leave for instep.
With RS of heel sts facing, rejoin yarn and cast on one st, k11 (12, 13), k2 tog, k11 (12, 13), turn and cast on one st.

Cont on these sts in st st for 4 cm/1½", ending with a p row.

Shape heel
1st row: K17 (19, 21), sl 1–k1 –psso, turn.
2nd row: Sl 1, p9 (11, 13), p2 tog, turn.
3rd row: Sl 1, k9 (11, 13), sl 1–k1–psso, turn.
Rep 2nd and 3rd rows 4 times more, then 2nd row again.
Break off yarn and sl rem 13 (15, 17) sts on to one needle. With RS facing, pick up and k11 sts along side of heel, k across sts on needle, then pick up and k11 sts along other side of heel. 35 (37, 39) sts.
Next row: P to end.
Next row: K1, sl 1–k1–psso, k to last 3 sts, k2 tog, k1.
Rep last 2 rows until 25 (27, 29) sts rem, then cont without shaping until work measures 6 (7, 8) cm/2½ (2¾, 3¼)" from where sts were picked up, ending with a p row.

Shape toe
Next row: K1, sl 1–k1–psso, k to last 3 sts, k2 tog, k1.
Next row: P to end.
Rep these 2 rows 2 (3, 4) times more, then first of them again.
Next row: P1, p2 tog, p to last 3 sts, p2 tog tb1, p1.
Break off yarn and leave rem 15 sts on st holder.
Return to instep sts and with larger needles and RS facing, rejoin yarn and work 10 (12, 14) rows in st st, then work "flower" motif in centre.
1st row: K10 (11, 12), yfwd/yo, k2 tog, k2, yfwd/yo, k2 tog, k9 (10, 11).
Work 3 rows.
5th row: K8 (9, 10), [yfwd/yo, k2 tog, k2] twice, yfwd/yo, k2 tog, k7 (8, 9).
Work 3 rows.
9th row: As 1st row.
Cont in st st until work measures same as under part of foot to beg of toe shaping, ending with a p row.
Shape toe as for under part of foot.

ASSEMBLY
Graft toe sts.
Join side seams of foot, then join back seam of leg.
Turn in hem at top on picot row and sew in place.
Press seams.

Chequerboard

MATERIALS
1 (1, 2) 25 g/1 oz balls (each approx 112 m/122 yds) of Twilleys *Lyscordet* (light weight cotton) in first colour (M)
2 (2, 3) balls in each of 4 other colours (A, B, C and D)
1 pair each of 2 mm/No 0 and 3 mm/No 3 knitting needles
4 buttons

MEASUREMENTS
To fit approx 6 (8, 10) years
Chest 66 (71, 76) cm/26 (28, 30)"
Length 42 (48, 54) cm/16½ (19, 21¼)"
Sleeve seam 25 (30, 35) cm/ 9¾ (11¾, 13¾)"

TENSION/GAUGE
28 sts and 36 rows to 10 cm/ 4" over st st using 3 mm/No 3 needles

BACK
With smaller needles and M, cast on 99 (107, 113) sts and work in k1, p1 rib for 4 cm/ 1½", ending with a WS row and inc one st in last row on 1st and 3rd sizes. 100 (107, 114) sts.
Change to larger needles and work in st st in patt as foll, using separate balls of each colour and twisting yarns where they join on every row to prevent holes:
1st row: K20 (22, 24) A, 20 (21, 22) B, 20 (21, 22) C, 20 (21, 22) D, 20 (22, 24) A.
Work 25 rows in colours as set.

27th row: K20 (22, 24) D, 20 (21, 22) C, 20 (21, 22) A, 20 (21, 22) B, 20 (22, 24) D.
Work 25 rows in colours as set.
53rd row: K20 (22, 24) B, 20 (21, 22) D, 20 (21, 22) B, 20 (21, 22) A, 20 (22, 24) C.
Work 25 rows in colours as set.
79th row: K20 (22, 24) C, 20 (21, 22) A, 20 (21, 22) D, 20 (21, 22) C, 20 (22, 24) B.
Work 25 rows in colours as set.
Beg again from 1st row and work in same sequence until work measures 42 (48, 54) cm/ 16½ (19, 21¼)" from beg, ending with a p row.

Shape shoulders
Cast/bind off 9 sts at beg of next 4 rows, then 8 (9, 10) sts at beg of next 4 rows.
Leave rem 32 (35, 38) sts on st holder.

FRONT
Work as for Back until work measures 37 (43, 49) cm/14½ (16½, 19¼)", ending with a p row.

Shape neck
Work in patt throughout and cont as foll:
Next row: K44 (47, 50), turn and leave rem sts on spare needle.
Cast/bind off 3 sts at beg of next row, 2 sts at beg of foll 3 alt rows, then one st at beg of foll 1 (2, 3) alt rows. 34 (36, 38) sts.
Cont without shaping until work measures as for Back to shoulders, ending with a p row.

Shape shoulder
Cast/bind off 9 sts at beg of next and foll alt row, then 8 (9, 10) sts at beg of foll alt row.
P 1 row, then cast/bind off rem 8 (9, 10) sts.
Return to sts on spare needle, sl first 12 (13, 14) sts on to st holder, rejoin yarn and k to end.
Cont to match first side, reversing shaping.

SLEEVES
With smaller needles and M, cast on 41 (45, 49) sts and work in k1, p1 rib for 4 cm/ 1½", ending with an RS row.
Next row: P1 (2, 3), p twice into each of next 39 (41, 43) sts, p1 (2, 3). 80 (86, 92) sts.

Change to larger needles and cont in st st, working in squares as foll:
1st row: K20 (22, 24) C, 20 (21, 22) A, 20 (21, 22) D, 20 (22, 24) C.
Work 25 rows in colours as set.
27th row: K20 (22, 24) B, 20 (21, 22) D, 20 (21, 22) B, 20 (22, 24) A.
Work 25 rows as set.
53rd row: K20 (22, 24) D, 20 (21, 22) C, 20 (21, 22) A, 20 (22, 24) B.
Work 25 rows as set.
79th row: K20 (22, 24) A, 20 (21, 22) B, 20 (21, 22) C, 20 (22, 24) D.
Work 25 rows as set.
Rep this sequence until sleeve measures 25 (30, 35) cm/9¾ (11¾, 13¾)", ending with a p row.
Cast/bind off.

NECKBAND
Join right shoulder seam.
With smaller needles, M, and RS facing, pick up and k24 (26, 28) sts down Left Front neck, k front neck sts, pick up and k23 (25, 27) sts up Right Front neck, then k back neck sts. 91 (99, 107) sts.
Work 8 rows in k1, p1 rib.
Cast/bind off in rib.
With smaller needles, M and RS facing, pick up and k27 sts along Left Back neckband and first 8 cm/3¼" of shoulder.
Work 4 rows in g st.
Cast/bind off.
Work along Left Front shoulder to match, making buttonholes on 2nd row by working k2, [cast/bind off 2 sts, k5] 3 times, cast/bind off 2 sts, k2.
On next row cast on 2 sts over each 2 cast/bound off.

ASSEMBLY
Press work according to instructions on yarn band.
Join rest of left shoulder seam. Sew in sleeves.
Join side and sleeve seams.
Press seams.
Sew on buttons.
Work embroidery as in picture (optional).

Cardigan

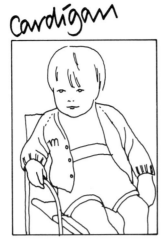

MATERIALS

4 25 g/1 oz balls (each approx 100 m/110 yds) of Robin *Landscape 4 ply* (4 ply/ fingering to sport weight yarn) in main colour (M)
2 balls in contrast colour (C)
1 pair each of 2¾ mm/No 2 and 3¼ mm/No 3 knitting needles
4 buttons for cardigan
4 buttons for shorts

MEASUREMENTS

To fit approx 12–18 months (18 months–2 years)
Chest 46 (51) cm/18 (20)″
Cardigan length 22 (24) cm/ 8¾ (9½)″
Sleeve seam 12 (14) cm/4¾ (5½)″
Shorts length (excluding straps) 27 (30) cm/10¾ (11¾)″

TENSION/GAUGE

26 sts and 38 rows to 10 cm/ 4″ over patt using 3¼ mm/ No 3 needles.

CARDIGAN

BACK

With smaller needles and M, cast on 63 (71) sts and work in k1, p1 rib for 3 cm/1¼″, ending with a WS row.
Change to larger needles and cont in patt as foll:
1st row: (RS) K3, *p1, k3, rep from * to end.
2nd row: P to end.
3rd row: K1, *p1, k3, rep from * to last 2 sts, p1, k1.
4th row: P to end.
Rep these 4 rows until work measures 13 (14) cm/5 (5½)″ from beg, ending with a p row.

Shape armholes

Cast/bind off 2 sts at beg of next 2 rows.

Next row: K1, sl 1–k1–psso, patt to last 3 sts, k2 tog, k1.
Next row: P to end.
Rep last 2 rows until 25 (27) sts rem, ending with a p row.
Cast/bind off.

LEFT FRONT

With smaller needles and M, cast on 31 (35) sts and work as for Back to armholes, ending with a p row.

Shape armhole and front edge

Cast/bind off 2 sts at beg of next row, then p 1 row.
Next row: K1, sl 1–k1–psso, patt to last 3 sts, k2 tog, k1.
Next row: P to end.
Rep last 2 rows until 9 (11) sts rem, then cont to dec at armhole edge only on every alt row until 2 sts rem, ending with a p row.
Cast/bind off.

RIGHT FRONT

Work to match Left Front, reversing all shaping.

SLEEVES

With smaller needles and M, cast on 35 (39) sts and work in k1, p1 rib for 3 cm/1¼″, ending with a WS row.
Change to larger needles and cont in patt as for Back, inc one st at each end of every 4th row until there are 47 (55) sts, then cont without shaping until sleeve measures 12 (14) cm/4¾ (5½)″, ending with a p row.

Shape top/cap

Cast/bind off 2 sts at beg of next 2 rows.
Dec as for Back armholes until 9 (11) sts rem, ending with a p row.
Cast/bind off.

FRONT BORDER

Join raglan seams.
With smaller needles and M, cast on 7 sts and work 4 rows in k1, p1 rib.
5th row: K1, p1, k1, yfwd/ yo, k2 tog, p1, k1.
Make 3 more buttonholes at equal intervals of approx 3 (4) cm/1¼ (1½)″, then cont until border is long enough to reach up front edge, around sleeve tops and back neck and down other front.
Cast/bind off.

ASSEMBLY

Press lightly according to instructions on yarn band.

Join side and sleeve seam.
Sew on front border.
Press seams.
Sew on buttons.

SHORTS

RIGHT LEG

With smaller needles and M, cast on 57 (65) sts and work in k1, p1 rib for 2 cm/¾″, ending with a WS row.
Break off M, join in C, change to larger needles and beg with a k row cont in st st for 2 cm/¾″, ending with a p row.
Cast on 2 sts at beg of next 4 rows.
Cont in st st, dec one st at each end of every 12th row until 55 (63) sts rem, then cont without shaping until work measures 23 (26) cm/9 (10¼)″ from beg, ending with a p row.
Break off C, join in M, change to smaller needles and k 1 row, then cont in rib as at beg for 7 rows.
Next row: Rib 13 (15), cast/ bind off 2 sts, rib to last 15 (17) sts, cast/bind off 2 sts, rib to end.
Next row: Rib to end, casting on 2 sts over each 2 cast/ bound off.
Work 6 more rows in rib, then cast/bind off loosely in rib.

LEFT LEG

Work as for Right Leg.

STRAPS (make 2)

With smaller needles and M, cast on 11 sts and work in k1, p1 rib for 36 (40) cm/14¼ (15¾)″, or length required.
Cast/bind off.

ASSEMBLY

Press work lightly according to instructions on yarn band.
Join back and front seams.
Join inside leg seams.
Press seams.
Sew a button to each end of each strap and fasten to waistband at back and front.

Frill Collar Top

MATERIALS
3 (4, 5) 50 g/$1\frac{3}{4}$ oz balls (each approx 105 m/115 yds) of Lister–Lee *Motoravia 4 ply* (4 ply/fingering to sport weight yarn) in main colour (M)
1 ball in contrast colour (C)
1 pair each of $2\frac{3}{4}$ mm/No 2 and $3\frac{1}{4}$ mm/No 3 needles
$3\frac{1}{4}$ mm/No 3 circular knitting needle
2.50 mm/size C crochet hook
3 buttons

MEASUREMENTS
To fit approx 4–6 (6–8, 8–10) years
Chest 61–66 (66–71, 71–76) cm/24–26 (26–28, 28–30)″
Length 35 (39, 43) cm/$13\frac{3}{4}$ ($15\frac{1}{2}$, 17)″
Sleeve seam 27 (30, 33) cm/ $10\frac{3}{4}$ ($11\frac{3}{4}$, 13)″

TENSION/GAUGE
28 sts and 36 rows to 10 cm/4″ over st st using $3\frac{1}{4}$ mm/No 3 needles.

BACK
With smaller needles and M, cast on 89 (95, 101) sts and work in k1, p1 rib for 6 cm/ $2\frac{1}{2}$″, ending with a WS row and inc 12 sts evenly across last row. 101 (107, 113) sts.
Change to larger needles and beg with a k row, cont in st st until work measures 22 (24, 26) cm/$8\frac{3}{4}$ ($9\frac{1}{2}$, $10\frac{1}{4}$)″ from beg, ending with a p row.

Shape armholes
Cast/bind off 4 sts at beg of next 2 rows, 3 sts at beg of next 2 rows, 2 sts at beg of next 2 rows, then dec one st at each end of next and foll alt row. 79 (85, 91) sts.
Cont without shaping until armholes measure 13 (15, 17) cm/5 (6, $6\frac{3}{4}$)″, ending with a p row.

Shape shoulders and neck
Next row: Cast/bind off 6 (7, 7) sts, k27 (28, 30) including st on needle, turn and leave rem sts on spare needle.
Next row: Cast/bind off 3 sts, p to end.
Next row: Cast/bind off 6 (7, 7) sts, k to end.
Rep last 2 rows once more.
Next row: Cast/bind off 2 sts, p to end.
Cast/bind off rem 7 (6, 8) sts.
Return to sts on spare needle, sl first 13 (15, 17) sts on to st holder for neck, rejoin yarn and k to end.
Cont to match first side, reversing shaping.

FRONT
Work as for Back until armhole shaping is completed, then cont without shaping until armholes measure 9 (11, 13) cm/$3\frac{1}{4}$ ($4\frac{1}{4}$, 5)″, ending with a p row.

Shape neck
Next row: K36 (38, 40), turn and leave rem sts on spare needle.
Cast/bind off 3 sts at beg of next row, then 2 sts at beg of foll alt row.
Dec one st at neck edge on next and foll 5 alt rows, ending with a p row.

Shape shoulders
Cast/bind off 6 (7, 7) sts at beg of next and foll 2 alt rows.
P 1 row, then cast/bind off rem 7 (6, 8) sts.
Return to sts on spare needle, sl first 7 (9, 11) sts on to st holder for neck, rejoin yarn and k to end.
Cont to match first side, reversing shaping.

SLEEVES
With smaller needles and M, cast on 51 (53, 55) sts and work in k1, p1 rib for 5 cm/2″, ending with a RS row.
Next row: Rib 3 (2, 1), *inc in next st, rib 2, rep from * to end. 67 (70, 73) sts.
Change to larger needles and cont in st st, inc one st at each end of every 18th row until there are 75 (78, 81) sts, then cont without shaping until sleeve measures 27 (30, 33) cm/$10\frac{3}{4}$ ($11\frac{3}{4}$, 13)″, ending with a p row.

Shape top/cap
Cast/bind off 3 sts at beg of next 2 rows, then 2 sts at beg of next 2 rows.
Dec at each end of next 2 rows, then work 1 row without shaping.
Rep last 3 rows until 25 (26, 27) sts rem, ending with a p row.
Cast/bind off 2 sts at beg of next 4 rows, then 3 sts at beg of next 2 rows.
Cast/bind off rem 11 (12, 13) sts.

COLLAR
With circular needle and C, cast on 362 (382, 402) sts and k4 rows, then cont in patt as foll:
1st row: P2, *k8, p2, rep from * to end.
2nd row: K2, *p8, k2, rep from * to end.
Rep these 2 rows 5 times more.
13th row: P2, *sl 1–k1–psso, k4, k2 tog, p2, rep from * to end.
14th row: K2, *p6, k2, rep from * to end.
15th row: P2, *sl 1–k1–psso, k2, k2 tog, p2, rep from * to end.
16th row: K2, *p4, k2, rep from * to end.
17th row: P2, *sl 1–k1–psso, k2 tog, p2, rep from * to end.
18th row: K2, *p2, k2, rep from * to end.
19th row: P2, *k2 tog, p2, rep from * to end.
20th row: K2, *p1, k2, rep from * to end.
21st row: P2 tog, *k1, p2 tog, rep from * to end. 73 (77, 81) sts.
Cast/bind off in rib.

ASSEMBLY
Press work according to instructions on yarn band.
Swiss darn/duplicate st dots as in picture.
With crochet hook and M, work 2 rows of dc/sc along Right Back shoulder, then work 2 rows along Right Front shoulder, making 3 button loops on 2nd row by working 2ch, miss/skip 1dc/sc, 1dc/sc into next dc/sc.
Join left shoulder seam.
Overlap Right Front shoulder over back and stitch at armhole edge.
Sew in sleeves.
Join side and sleeve seams.
Sew on collar, beg and ending at right shoulder.
Press seams.
Sew on buttons.

Soft Stripes Collar

MATERIALS
5 (5, 6) 25 g/1 oz balls (each approx 53.25 m/58.5 yds) of Argyll *Finesse* (medium weight mohair) in main colour (M)
2 (3, 3) balls in contrast colour (C)
1 pair each of $4\frac{1}{2}$ mm/No 7 and $5\frac{1}{2}$ mm/No 9 knitting needles
3 buttons

MEASUREMENTS
To fit approx 2 (4, 6) years
Chest 56 (61, 66) cm/22 (24, 26)″
Length 35 (39, 43) cm/$13\frac{3}{4}$ ($15\frac{1}{4}$, 17)″
Sleeve seam 33 (36, 39) cm/ 13 ($14\frac{1}{4}$, $15\frac{1}{4}$)″

TENSION/GAUGE
16 sts and 22 rows to 10 cm/ 4″ over st st using $5\frac{1}{2}$ mm/ No 9 needles.

BACK
With smaller needles and C, cast on 47 (51, 55) sts.
1st row: K1, *p1, k1, rep from * to end.
2nd row: P1, *k1, p1, rep from * to end.
Rep these 2 rows for 5 cm/ 2″, ending with a 2nd row and inc 5 sts evenly across last row. 52 (56, 60) sts.
Change to larger needles, join in M and cont in st st, work 12 rows in M, 8 rows in C, then cont in M until work measures 24 (26, 28) cm/$19\frac{1}{2}$ ($10\frac{1}{4}$, 11)″, ending with a p row.

Shape armholes
Cast/bind off 4 sts at beg of next 2 rows. 44 (48, 52) sts.
Cont without shaping until armholes measure 11 (13, 15) cm/$4\frac{1}{4}$ (5, 6)″, ending with a p row.
Next row: Cast/bind off 13

(14, 15) sts, k until there are 18 (20, 22) sts on RH needle, cast/bind off rem 13 (14, 15) sts.
Leave sts on st holder.

FRONT
Work as for Back until armhole shaping is completed, then work 0 (2, 4) rows.

Divide for front opening
Next row: K20 (22, 24), turn and leave rem sts on spare needle.
Cont on these sts, work 12 rows, ending at neck edge.

Shape neck
Cast/bind off 3 (3, 4) sts at beg of next row, then dec one st at neck edge on every row until 13 (14, 15) sts rem.
Cont without shaping until armhole measures as for Back, ending with a p row.
Cast/bind off.
Return to sts on spare needle, with RS facing, rejoin yarn and cast/bind off 4 sts, k to end.
Cont to match first side.

SLEEVES
With smaller needles and C, cast on 21 (23, 25) sts and work in rib as for Back for 5 cm/2″, ending with a 2nd row and inc 3 sts evenly across last row. 24 (26, 28) sts.
Break off C, join in M, change to larger needles and cont in st st, inc one st at each end of every 8th row until there are 36 (40, 44) sts, then cont without shaping until sleeve measures 33 (36, 39) cm/13 (14$\frac{1}{4}$, 15$\frac{1}{4}$)″, ending with a p row.
Place a marker at each end of last row, then work a further 2.5 cm/1″.
Cast/bind off loosely.

BUTTONHOLE BORDER
With smaller needles and C, pick up and k15 sts along right edge of front opening for Girl or left edge for Boy.
K 1 row, then beg with p1, work 1 row in rib as at beg.
Next row: K1, p1, k1, [yfwd/ yo, k2 tog, p1, k1] 3 times.
Work 2 more rows in rib, then cast/bind off in rib.

BUTTON BORDER
Work to match buttonhole border, omitting buttonholes.

COLLAR
With smaller needles and C, cast on 59 (65, 71) sts and work in rib as foll:
1st row: K2, *p1, k1, rep from * to last st, k1.
2nd row: K1, *p1, k1, rep from * to end.
Rep these 2 rows for 8 cm/ 3$\frac{1}{4}$″, ending with a 2nd row.
Cast/bind off loosely in rib.

ASSEMBLY
Press work according to instructions on yarn band.
Join shoulder seams.
Sew in sleeves, sewing last part of sleeve seams to cast/ bound off sts at armholes.
Join side and sleeve seams.
Sew down edges of front borders.
Sew on collar, beg and ending in centre of front borders.
Press seams.
Sew on buttons.

Soft Stripes Shoulder Fastening

MATERIALS
5 (5, 6) 25 g/1 oz balls (each approx 53.25 m/58.5 yds) of Argyll *Finesse* (medium weight mohair) in main colour (M)
2 (2, 3) balls in contrast colour (C)
1 pair each of 4$\frac{1}{2}$ mm/No 7 and 5$\frac{1}{2}$ mm/No 9 needles
3 buttons

MEASUREMENTS
To fit approx 2 (4, 6) years
Chest 56 (61, 66) cm/22 (24, 26)″
Length 38 (42, 46) cm/15 (16$\frac{1}{2}$, 18)″
Sleeve seam 33 (36, 39) cm/ 13 (14$\frac{1}{4}$, 15$\frac{1}{4}$)″

TENSION/GAUGE
16 sts and 22 rows to 10 cm/ 4″ over st st using 5$\frac{1}{2}$ mm/ No 9 needles.

BACK
With smaller needles and C, cast on 47 (51, 55) sts.
1st row: K1, *p1, k1, rep from * to end.
2nd row: P1, *k1, p1, rep from * to end.
Rep these 2 rows for 5 cm/ 2″, ending with a 2nd row and inc 5 sts evenly across last row. 52 (56, 60) sts.
Break off C.
Change to larger needles, join in M and cont in st st until work measures 26 (28, 30) cm/10$\frac{1}{4}$ (11, 11$\frac{3}{4}$)″, ending with a p row.

Shape armholes
Cast/bind off 4 sts at beg of next 2 rows. 44 (48, 52) sts.
Cont without shaping until armholes measure 12 (14, 16) cm/4$\frac{3}{4}$ (5$\frac{1}{2}$, 6$\frac{1}{4}$)″, ending with a p row.

Shape shoulders
Cast/bind off 13 (14, 15) sts at beg of next 2 rows.
Leave rem 18 (20, 22) sts on st holder.

FRONT
Work as for Back until armhole shaping is completed, ending with a p row.

Divide for front opening
1st row: K to last 2 sts, k2 tog.
2nd row: P2 tog, p to end.
Rep these 2 rows once more, then 1st row again. 39 (43, 47) sts.
6th row: P to end.
7th row: As 1st row.
Rep last 2 rows 2 (3, 4) times more, then 6th row again.

Shape neck
Next row: K17 (18, 20), k2 tog, turn and leave rem sts on spare needle.
Dec one st at neck edge on next 3 (3, 5) rows, then on every other row until 13 (14, 15) sts rem.
Cont without shaping until armhole measures as for Back, ending with a p row.
Cast/bind off.
Return to sts on spare needle, sl first 6 (8, 8) sts on to st holder and rejoin yarn.
Next row: K2 tog, k to last 2 sts, k2 tog.
Next row: P to end.
Rep last 2 rows 3 times more, then cont to dec at armhole edge only on every other row until 2 sts rem.
Cast/bind off.

FRONT UNDERLAP
With smaller needles and C, cast on 3 sts and work in st st, inc one st at beg of 3rd and every alt row until there are 13 (14, 15) sts, then work 7 rows.
Cast/bind off.

LEFT SLEEVE
With smaller needles and C, cast on 23 (25, 27) sts and work in rib as for Back for 5 cm/2″, ending with a 2nd row and inc 3 sts evenly across last row. 26 (28, 30) sts.
Break off C, join in M, change to larger needles and cont in st st, inc one st at each end of 3rd and every foll 8th row until there are 40 (44, 48) sts, then cont without shaping until sleeve measures 33 (36, 39) cm/13 (14¼, 15¼)″ from beg, ending with a p row.
Place a marker at each end of last row, then work a further 2.5 cm/1″.
Cast/bind off.

RIGHT SLEEVE
Work as for Left Sleeve, but using M instead of C and C instead of M.

NECKBAND
Join left shoulder seam.
Sew cast/bound off edge of front underlap to right back shoulder.
With smaller needles and C, pick up and k7 sts up neck edge of underlap, k back neck sts, then pick up and k28 (30, 30) sts around front neck, including sts on st holder. 53 (57, 59) sts.
K 1 row.
Work in rib as for Back for 2.5 cm/1″.
Cast/bind off in rib.

BUTTONHOLE BORDER
With smaller needles, C and RS facing, pick up and k30 sts along shaped front edge.

K 1 row.
Next row: K2, *p1, k1, rep from * to end.
Next row: P2 tog, rib 4, [yfwd/yo, k2 tog, rib 8] twice, yfwd/yo, k2 tog, rib 2.
Work 2 more rows in rib, dec at bottom edge on each row.
Cast/bind off in rib.

ASSEMBLY
Press work according to instructions on yarn band.
Lap shaped edge of buttonhole border over bottom of underlap and stitch in place.
Sew in sleeves.
Join side and sleeve seams.
Press seams.
Sew on buttons.

MATERIALS
3 (4, 4, 5, 5, 6) 50 g/1¾ oz balls (each approx 125 m/140 yds) of Pingouin *Confort* (double knitting/sport to knitting worsted weight yarn) in main colour (M)
1 ball in each of 2 contrast colours (A and B)
1 pair each of 3 mm/No 3 and 3¾ mm/No 5 knitting needles
Set of four 3 mm/No 3 double-pointed knitting needles

MEASUREMENTS
To fit approx 2 (4, 6, 8, 10, 12) years
Chest 56 (61, 66, 71, 76, 81) cm/22 (24, 26, 28, 30, 32)″
Length 29 (33, 37, 41, 45, 49) cm/11¼ (13, 14½, 16¼, 17¾, 19¼)″
Sleeve seam 21 (25, 29, 33, 47, 41) cm/8¼ (9¾, 11½, 13, 14½, 16¼)″

TENSION/GAUGE
22 sts and 28 rows to 10 cm/4″ over st st using 3¾ mm/No 5 needles.

BACK
With smaller needles and M, cast on 59 (65, 71, 77, 83, 89) sts and work in k1, p1 rib for 8 cm/3¼″, ending with a WS row and inc 7 sts evenly across last row. 66 (72, 78, 84, 90, 96) sts.
Change to larger needles and cont in st st, work 6 rows M, 2 rows A, 2 rows M, 2 rows B, then cont in M until work measures 10 (11, 12, 13, 14, 15) cm/4 (4¼, 4¾, 5, 5½, 6)″ from beg, ending with a p row.
Next row: K4 (7, 10, 13, 16, 19) M, work 58 sts of 1st row of "GOODBYE" chart using B and M and reading chart from right to left, then k to end in M only.
Cont foll chart and when 10 rows of chart have been completed, cont in M until work measures 18 (21, 24, 27, 30, 33) cm/7 (8¼, 9½, 10¾, 11¾, 13)″ from beg, ending with a p row.

Shape armholes
Cast/bind off 3 sts at beg of next 2 rows, then 2 sts at beg of next 0 (0, 2, 2, 4, 4) rows.**
Dec one st at each end of next and every other row until 54 (56, 60, 62, 66, 68) sts rem.
Cont without shaping until armholes measure 11 (12, 13, 14, 15, 16) cm/4¼ (4¾, 5, 5½, 6, 6¼)″, ending with a p row.

Shape shoulders
Cast/bind off 4 (5, 5, 5, 6, 6) sts at beg of next 4 rows, then 5 (4, 5, 6, 5, 6) sts at beg of next 2 rows.
Leave rem 28 (28, 30, 30, 32, 32) sts on st holder.

FRONT
Work as for Back, omitting "GOODBYE" motif, as far as **. 60 (66, 68, 74, 76, 82) sts.
Next row: K2 tog, k10 (13, 14, 17, 18, 21) M, work 36 sts of 1st row of "HELLO" chart using A and M, then using M only, k to last 2 sts, k2 tog.
Dec at each end of every other row until 54 (56, 60, 62, 66, 68) sts rem, and AT THE

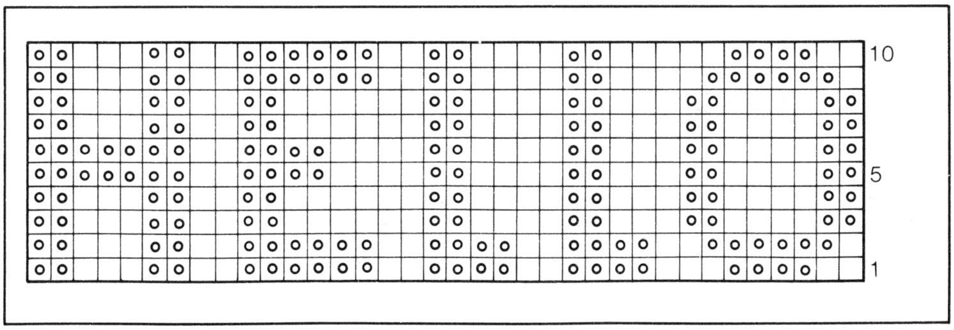

Chart for sweater front

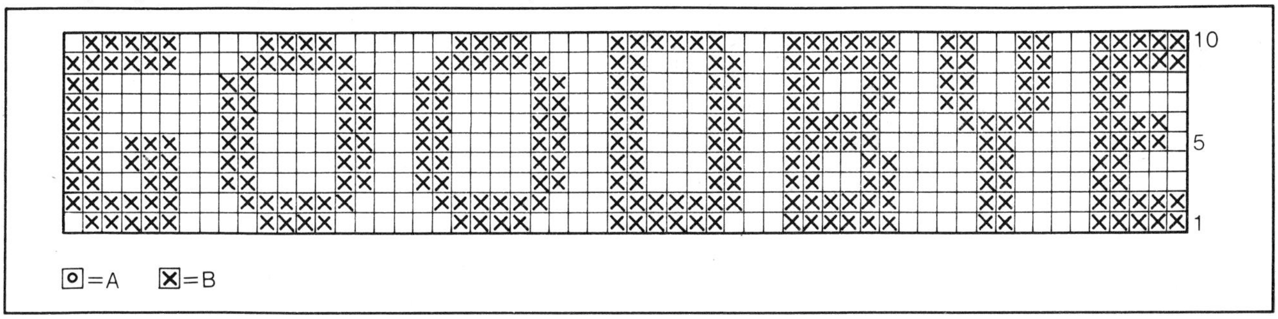

○ = A   × = B

Chart for sweater back, worked in stocking/stockingette stitch.

97

SAME TIME cont with motif until 10 rows of chart have been completed, then cont in M until armholes measure 7 (8, 9, 9, 10, 11) cm/2¾ (3¼, 3½, 3½, 4, 4¼)″, ending with a p row.

Shape neck
Next row: K19 (20, 21, 22, 23, 24), turn and leave rem sts on a spare needle.
Dec one st at neck edge on every other row until 13 (14, 15, 16, 17, 18) sts rem, then cont without shaping until armholes measure as for Back, ending with a p row.

Shape shoulders
Cast/bind off 4 (5, 5, 5, 6, 6) sts at beg of next and foll alt row.
P 1 row, then cast/bind off rem 5 (4, 5, 6, 5, 6) sts.
Return to sts on spare needle, sl first 16 (16, 18, 18, 20, 20) sts on to st holder for neck, rejoin yarn and k to end.
Cont to match first side.

SLEEVES
With smaller needles and M, cast on 33 (35, 35, 37, 37, 39) sts and work in k1, p1 rib for 5 cm/2″, ending with a WS row and inc one st in last row. 34 (36, 36, 38, 38, 40) sts.
Change to larger needles and cont in st st, inc one st at each end of next and every foll 6th (7th, 7th, 8th, 7th, 8th) row until there are 48 (50, 54, 56, 60, 62) sts, but AT THE SAME TIME when sleeve measures 16 (20, 24, 27, 31, 35) cm/6¼ (7¾, 9½, 10¾, 12¼, 13¾)″ from beg, work stripes of 2 rows A, 2 rows M, 2 rows B, 2 rows M, 2 rows A, 2 rows M, 2 rows B, then cont in M until sleeve measures 21 (25, 29, 33, 37, 41) cm/8¼ (9¾, 11½, 13, 14½, 16¼)″, ending with a p row.

Shape top/cap
Cast/bind off 3 sts at beg of next 2 rows.
Dec one st at each end of next and every other row until 26 (26, 28, 28, 30, 30) sts rem, ending with a p row.
Cast/bind off 2 sts at beg of next 4 rows, then 2 (2, 3, 3, 4, 4) sts at beg of next 2 rows.
Cast/bind off rem 14 sts.

NECKBAND
Join shoulder seams.
With set of four double-pointed needles, M and RS facing, pick up and k14 (14, 14, 16, 16, 16) sts down Left Front neck, k front neck sts, pick up and k14 (14, 14, 16, 16, 16) sts up Right Front neck, then k back neck sts. 72 (72, 76, 80, 84, 84) sts.
Work 15 rounds in k1, p1 rib.
Cast/bind off loosely in rib.

ASSEMBLY
Press work according to instructions on yarn band.
Sew in sleeves.
Join side and sleeve seams.
Fold neckband in half to inside and sew in place.
Press seams.

MATERIALS
1 (2, 2) 50 g/1¾ oz balls (each approx 133 m/145 yds) of Phildar *Sagittaire 245* (double knitting/sport weight yarn) in 1st colour (A)
1 ball each in 2nd, 3rd, 4th and 5th colours (B, C, D and E)
1 pair of 6 mm/No 10 knitting needles

MEASUREMENTS
To fit approx 2 (4, 6) years
Chest 56(61,66) cm/22(24,26)″
Length 34 (39, 44) cm/13½ (15¼, 17¼)″
Sleeve seam 21 (23, 25) cm/8¼ (9, 9¾)″

TENSION/GAUGE
16 sts and 20 rows to 10 cm/4″ over st st using 6 mm/No 10 needles and 2 strands of yarn.

Note: Yarn is used double throughout.

BACK
With A, cast on 44 (48, 52) sts.
K 6 rows.
Beg with a k row, work stripes in st st as foll:

10 rows in B.
10 rows in C.
10 rows in D.
10 rows in E.
Rep the 1st 20 (30, 40) rows again.
Using A, k 6 rows.
Cast/bind off in A.

FRONT
Work as for Back.

SLEEVES
With A, cast on 50 sts.
K 6 rows.
Beg with a k row, work in st st as foll:
7 rows in B.
7 rows in C.
6 rows in D.
6 rows in A.
6 rows in E.
6 (10, 14) rows in A.
Cast/bind off in A.

ASSEMBLY
Join shoulder seams for 8 cm/3¼″ from armhole edge.
Sew cast/bound-off edges of sleeves to armhole edges of body.
Join side and sleeve seams.
Press lightly foll instructions on yarn band.

MATERIALS
4 (5, 6) 50 g/1¾ oz balls (each approx 183 m/200 yds) of Lister–Lee *Motoravia 4 ply* (4 ply/fingering to sport weight yarn) in main colour (M)
2 (2, 3) balls in contrast colour (C)
1 pair each of 2¾ mm/No 2 and 3¼ mm/No 3 needles
4 buttons

MEASUREMENTS
To fit approx 2 (4, 6) years
Chest 56 (61, 66) cm/22 (24, 26)″
Length 53 (58, 64) cm/20¾ (22¾, 25¼)″
Sleeve seam 25 (29, 33) cm/

$9\frac{3}{4}$ ($11\frac{1}{2}$, 13)"

TENSION/GAUGE
28 sts and 36 rows to 10 cm/ 4" over st st using $3\frac{1}{4}$ mm/ No 3 needles.

BACK
With smaller needles and M, cast on 124 (130, 136) sts and beg with a k row, work 7 rows in st st, then k 1 row to mark hemline.
Change to larger needles and cont in patt as foll:
1st row: K to end in M.
2nd row: P to end in M.
3rd row: *K1M, 1C, rep from * to end.
4th row: As 2nd row.
5th row: As 1st row.
6th row: *P1M, 1C, rep from * to end. These 6 rows form patt and are rep throughout. Cont in patt until work measures 36 (38, 41) cm/$14\frac{1}{4}$ (15, $16\frac{1}{4}$)" from hemline, ending with a 6th row.
Next row: With M, k0 (3, 6), k2 tog, *k1, k2 tog, rep from * to last 2 (5, 8) sts, k2 tog, k0 (3, 6). 82 (88, 94) sts.
Cont in patt until work measures 41 (45, 50) cm/$16\frac{1}{4}$ ($17\frac{3}{4}$, $19\frac{3}{4}$)" from hemline, ending with a p row.

Shape armholes
Keeping patt correct, cast/ bind off 2 (3, 4) sts at beg of next 2 rows, then dec one st at each end of next and every other row until 72 (76, 80) sts rem, ending with a p row.**

Divide for back opening
Keep patt correct throughout and work as foll:
Next row: K33 (35, 37) sts in patt, k6M, turn, leave rem sts on spare needle.
Next row: K6M, p to end in patt.
Keeping 6 sts at inside edge in g st in M throughout, work 2 rows.
Next row: (buttonhole row) Work to last 4 sts, yfwd/yo, k2 tog, k2.
Cont as set, work 2 more buttonholes on every 12th (14th, 16th) row, then work 5 rows.

Shape shoulder
Cast/bind off 8 sts at beg of next and foll alt row, then 8 (9, 10) sts at beg of foll alt row.
Leave rem 15 (16, 17) sts on st holder. Return to sts on spare needle, using M, cast on 6

sts, then with RS facing, k across rem sts in patt.
Next row: P in patt to last 6 sts, k6M. Cont to match first side, omitting buttonholes and reversing shaping.

FRONT
Work as for Back to **, then cont without shaping until work is 4 cm/$1\frac{1}{2}$" less than Back to shoulders, ending with a p row.

Shape neck
Next row: K30 (31, 32), turn and leave rem sts on spare needle.
Dec one st at neck edge on every row until 24 (25, 26) sts rem, then cont without shaping until armhole measures as for Back, ending with a p row.

Shape shoulder
Cast/bind off 8 sts at beg of next and foll alt row.
P 1 row, then cast/bind off rem 8 (9, 10) sts.
Return to sts on spare needle, sl first 12 (14, 16) sts on to st holder, rejoin yarn and k to end.
Cont to match first side, reversing shaping.

SLEEVES
With smaller needles and M, cast on 43 (49, 55) sts and work in k1, p1 rib for 4 cm/ $1\frac{1}{2}$", ending with a WS row and inc 13 (15, 17) sts evenly across last row. 56 (64, 72) sts.
Change to larger needles and cont in patt as for Back until sleeve measures 25 (29, 33) cm/$9\frac{3}{4}$ ($11\frac{1}{2}$, 13)" from beg, ending with a p row.

Shape top/cap
Keeping patt correct, cast/ bind off 2 (3, 4) sts at beg of next 2 rows, then dec one st at each end of every row until 12 sts rem.
Cast/bind off.

NECKBAND
Join shoulder seams.
With smaller needles, M and RS facing k15 (16, 17) sts of Left Back neck, pick up ,and k23 sts down Left Front neck, k front neck sts, pick up and k23 sts up Right Front neck, then k sts of Right Back neck. 88 (92, 96) sts.
Work 3 rows in g st.
Next row: K to last 4 sts, yfwd/yo, k2 tog, k2.

Work 4 more rows in g st, then cast/bind off.

RUFFLE (make 2 pieces)
With larger needles and M, cast on 126 (156, 186) sts and work in patt as 1st–6th rows of Back for 16 rows.
Next row: Using M, *k1, k2 tog, rep from * to end.
Cast/bind off in M.

BAG (make 2 pieces)
With larger needles and M, cast on 20 sts.
1st row: *K1M, 1C, rep from * to end.
2nd row: *P1C, 1M, rep from * to end. Keeping patt correct as set, inc one st at each end of next and every other row until there are 28 sts, then cont until work measures 9 cm/$3\frac{1}{2}$" from beg, ending with a p row.
Next row: Using M, *k2, yfwd/yo, k2 tog, rep from * to end.
Next row: Using M, p to end.
Work 4 rows in patt as at beg.
Cast/bind off.

ASSEMBLY
Press work according to instructions on yarn band.
Sew in sleeves.
Join side and sleeve seams.
Turn up hem at lower edge and sew in place.
Sew button band inside buttonhole band at cast on edge.
Sew on ruffle as in picture.
Sew on buttons.
Press seams.
Join sides and lower edge of bag. Make a twisted cord and thread through holes at top, gather and stitch to dress at waist.

MATERIALS
1 (2, 3) 25 g/1 oz balls (each

approx 183 m/200 yds) of Lister–Lee *Motoravia 4 ply* (4 ply/fingering to sport weight yarn) in 1st colour (A)
2 (3, 3) balls in 2nd colour (B)
2 (2, 3) balls in 3rd colour (C)
1 (1, 2) balls in 4th colour (D)
1 pair each of $2\frac{3}{4}$ mm/No 2 and $3\frac{1}{4}$ mm/No 3 knitting needles
30 (35, 35) cm/12 (14, 14)" zipper

MEASUREMENTS
To fit approx 6 (12, 18) months
Chest 46 (51, 56) cm/18 (20, 22)"
Length from back neck to ankle 54 (61, 70) cm/$21\frac{1}{4}$ (24, $27\frac{1}{2}$)"
Sleeve seam 16 (18, 22) cm/ $6\frac{1}{4}$ (7, $8\frac{3}{4}$)"

TENSION/GAUGE
28 sts and 50 rows to 10 cm/ 4" over g st using $3\frac{1}{4}$ mm/ No 3 needles.

SUIT

BACK
With larger needles and B, cast on 30 (32, 34) sts.

Left leg
Work in g st for 12 (14, 17) cm/ $4\frac{3}{4}$ ($5\frac{1}{2}$, $6\frac{3}{4}$)", ending with a WS row. Inc one st at beg of next and every 4th row until there are 36 (38, 40) sts, then cont without shaping until work measures 17 (19, 22) cm/ $6\frac{3}{4}$ ($7\frac{1}{2}$, $8\frac{3}{4}$)", ending with a WS row.**
Leave sts on spare needle, but do not break off yarn.

Right leg
Using C, work as for Left Leg, reversing shaping and ending with a WS row.

Join legs
Next row: Using C, k36 (38, 40) sts of Right Leg, then using B, k across sts of Left Leg. 72 (76, 80) sts.
Cont in g st in colours as set, twisting colours where they join on every row, until work measures 25 (32, 37) cm/$9\frac{3}{4}$ ($12\frac{1}{2}$, $14\frac{1}{2}$)", ending with a WS row and dec one st in centre of last row. 71 (75, 79) sts.
Change to smaller needles and A.
Next row: K1, *p1, k1, rep from * to end.
Next row: P1, *k1, p1, rep from * to end.

99

Rep these 2 rows for 3 cm/1¼", ending with a WS row and inc one st in centre of last row. 72 (76, 80) sts.

Change to larger needles and cont in g st as foll:

Next row: K36 (38, 40) A, 36 (38, 40) D. Cont in colours as set until work measures 38 (46, 53) cm/15 (18, 20¾)" from beg, ending with a WS row.

Shape armholes

Cast/bind off 2 sts at beg of next 4 rows, then dec one st at each end of next and every other row until 60 (64, 68) sts rem.

Cont in colours as set until work measures 47 (56, 64) cm/18½ (22, 25¼)" from beg, ending with a WS row.

Shape shoulders and neck

Next row: Cast/bind off 5 sts, k19 (20, 21) including st on needle, turn and leave rem sts on spare needle.

Next row: Cast/bind off 2 sts, k to end.

Next row: Cast/bind off 5 sts, k to last 2 sts, k2 tog.

Next row: K to end.

Rep last 2 rows once more, then cast/bind off rem 5 (6, 7) sts.

Return to sts on spare needle, sl first 12 (14, 16) sts on to st holder, rejoin yarn and k to end.

Cont to match first side.

RIGHT FRONT

With larger needles and C, work as for Left Back Leg to **, then cont in g st until work measures 25 (32, 37) cm/9¾ (12½, 14½)" from beg, ending with a WS row and dec one st in last row. 35 (37, 39) sts.

Change to smaller needles and A and work in rib as for Back for 3 cm/1¼", ending with a WS row and inc one st in last row. 36 (38, 40) sts.

Change to larger needles and still using A, cont in g st until work measures 38 (46, 53) cm/15 (18, 20¾)" from beg, ending with an RS row.

Shape armhole

Cast/bind off 2 sts at beg of next and foll alt row, then dec one st at beg of every other row until 30 (32, 34) sts rem.

Cont without shaping until work measures 45 (53, 60) cm/17¾ (20¾, 23½)" from beg, ending with a WS row.

Shape neck

Cast/bind off 3 sts at beg of next row, then 2 sts at beg of foll alt row.

Work 1 row.

Dec one st at neck edge on next and every foll 3rd row until 20 (21, 22) sts rem, then cont without shaping until work measures as for Back to shoulder, ending at armhole edge.

Shape shoulder

Cast/bind off 5 sts at beg of next and foll 2 alt rows.

K 1 row, then cast/bind off rem 5 (6, 7) sts.

LEFT FRONT

Work to match Right Front, reversing all shaping and using B instead of C and D instead of A.

SLEEVES (both alike)

With smaller needles and B, cast on 43 (45, 47) sts and work in rib as for Back waist for 4 cm/1½", ending with a WS row and inc 4 sts evenly in last row. 47 (49, 51) sts.

Change to larger needles and cont in g st, inc one st at each end of every 10th (8th, 6th) row until there are 57 (65, 71) sts.

Cont without shaping until sleeve measures 16 (18, 22) cm/6¼ (7, 8¾)" from beg, ending with a WS row.

Shape top/cap

Cast/bind off 2 sts at beg of next 2 rows.

Dec one st at each end of next 2 rows, then work 1 row without shaping.

Rep last 3 rows 7 (9, 11) times more, then dec one st at each end of next row on 1st and 2nd sizes only and k 1 row. 19 sts.

Cast/bind off 2 sts at beg of next 2 rows, then 3 sts at beg of next 2 rows. Cast/bind off rem 9 sts.

NECKBAND

Join shoulder seams.

With smaller needles, A and RS facing, pick up and k19 (23, 27) sts up Right Front neck and 3 sts down Right Back neck, k back neck sts inc one st in centre, then pick up and k3 sts up Left Back neck and 19 (23, 27) sts down Left Front neck.

Work in k1, p1 rib for 3 cm/1¼".

Cast/bind off in rib.

ASSEMBLY

Do not press.

Sew in sleeves.

Join side and sleeve seams.

With smaller needles, A and RS facing, pick up and k45 (47, 51) sts along lower edge of leg.

Work in k1, p1 rib for 4 cm/1½".

Cast/bind off in rib.

Join inside leg seams.

Join front seams for approx 1 (2, 3) cm/½ (¾, 1¼)".

Sew in zipper, adjusting seam below it if necessary.

HAT

EARFLAPS (make 2)

With larger needles and C, cast on 3 sts and k 1 row.

Cont in g st, cast on 2 sts at beg of next 4 rows, then inc one st at each end of next and every 4th row until there are 15 (17, 19) sts.

Cont without shaping until work measures 5 (6, 7) cm/2 (2½, 2¾)", ending with a WS row.

Cast/bind off.

MAIN PART

With larger needles and A, cast on 97 (103, 109) sts and work 30 (36, 40) rows in g st, then break off A.

Join in B and C and work 2 rows B, 2 rows C.

Shape top

Still working in stripe patt as set, cont as foll:

Next row: K1, *k2 tog, k4, rep from * to end.

K 3 rows.

Next row: K1, *k2 tog, k3, rep from * to end.

K 3 rows.

Cont to dec in this way on next and foll 4th row, then k 3 rows. 33 (35, 37) sts.

Next row: K2 tog to last st, k1.

Break off yarn, thread through sts, gather up and fasten off.

ASSEMBLY

Do not press.

Join back seam.

Sew on earflaps.

Make a small pom pon in C and sew to top of hat.

Make 2 ties in C and sew to earflaps to tie under chin.

Country Jumper

MATERIALS
3 (4) 50 g/1¾ oz balls (each approx 120 m/131 yds) of Patons *Clansman DK* (double knitting/sport to knitting worsted weight yarn) in main colour (M)
1 ball in each of 2 contrast colours (A and B)
1 pair each of 3¼ mm/No 3 and 4 mm/No 6 knitting needles
3.50 mm/size E crochet hook
3 small buttons

MEASUREMENTS
To fit approx 2–4 (4–6) years
Chest 56 (61) cm/22 (24)″
Length 34 (39) cm/13½ (15¼)″
Sleeve seam 24 (27) cm/9½ (10¾)″

TENSION/GAUGE
23 sts and 26 rows to 10 cm/4″ over Fair Isle patt using 4 mm/No 6 needles.

BACK
With smaller needles, cast on 71 (77) sts and work in k1, p1 rib for 7 cm/2¾″, ending with a WS row and inc 2 (3) sts in last row. 73 (80) sts.
Change to larger needles and beg with a k row, work 2 rows in st st, then cont in patt:
1st row: (RS) K1M, *1A, 6M, rep from * to last 2 sts, 1A, 1M.
2nd row: P2M, *1A, 4M, 1A, 1M, rep from * to last st, 1M.
3rd row: K3M, *1A, 2M, 1A, 3M, rep from * to end.
4th row: P to end in M.
Rep these 4 rows until work measures approx 20 (22) cm/7¾ (8¾)″ from beg, ending with a 4th patt row and dec one st in last row on 2nd size only. 73 (79) sts.
Work first 8 rows of patt from chart, reading odd num-bered rows from right to left and even rows left to right.

Shape armholes
Still working in patt from chart, cast/bind off 3 sts at beg of next 2 rows, 2 (3) sts at beg of next 2 rows, 2 sts at beg of next 2 rows, then one st at beg of next 2 rows. 57 (61) sts. This completes 16 rows of patt.
Work 2 rows in st st, inc one st in last row on 2nd size only. 57 (62) sts.
Next row: K1 (0) A, *6M, 1A, rep from * to last 0 (6) sts, 0 (6) M.
This sets position of patt as on lower part.
Cont in patt until armholes measure 11 (14) cm/4¼ (5½)″, ending with a p row.

Shape shoulders and neck
Cast/bind off 6 sts at beg of next 2 rows.
Next row: Cast/bind off 5 (6) sts, k until there are 5 sts on RH needle, turn and p 1 row.
Cast/bind off.
Sl next 25 (28) sts on to st holder, rejoin yarn to rem 10 (11) sts and k to end.
Cast/bind off 5 (6) sts at beg of next row.
K 1 row, then cast/bind off rem 5 sts.

FRONT
Work as for Back until arm-holes measure 5 (8) cm/2 (3¼)″, ending with a p row.

Shape neck
Next row: K23 (24), turn and leave rem sts on spare needle.

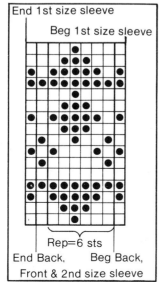

```
End 1st size sleeve
        Beg 1st size sleeve
```

```
            Rep=6 sts
End Back,        Beg Back,
Front & 2nd size sleeve
```

Chart for Country sweater

Cast/bind off 3 sts at beg of next row, then 2 sts at beg of foll 2 alt rows. 16 (17) sts.
Cont without shaping until armhole measures as for Back, ending with a p row.

Shape shoulder
Cast/bind off 6 sts at beg of next row, then 5 (6) sts at beg of foll alt row.
Work 1 row, then cast/bind off rem 5 sts.
Return to sts on spare needle, sl first 11 (14) sts on to st holder for neck, rejoin yarn and k to end.
Cont to match first side.

SLEEVES
With smaller needles and M, cast on 35 (37) sts and work in k1, p1 rib for 6 cm/2½″, ending with a WS row and inc 7 sts evenly in last row. 42 (44) sts.
Change to larger needles and work 2 rows in st st, then cont in patt as foll:
1st row: K3 (4) M, *1A, 6M, rep from * to last 4 (5) sts, 1A, 3 (4) M.
2nd row: P2 (3) M, *1A, 1M, 1A, 4M, rep from * to last 5 (6) sts, 1A, 1M, 1A, 2 (3) M.
3rd row: K1 (2) M, *1A, 3M, 1A, 2M, rep from * to last 6 (7) sts, 1A, 3M, 1A, 1 (2) M.
4th row: P to end in M.
Cont in patt, inc one st at each end of next and every foll 4th row, working extra sts into patt, until there are 56 (60) sts, then cont without shaping until sleeve measures 21 (24) cm/8¼ (9½)″ from beg, ending with a 4th patt row and inc one st in last row.
Work first 8 rows of patt from chart.

Shape top/cap
Still working in patt, cast/bind off 3 sts at beg of next 2 rows, then dec one st at each end of next and foll 2 alt rows, ending with a p row. 45 (49) sts. This completes patt.
Work 2 rows in st st, dec one st at each end of each row and one st in centre of 2nd row. 40 (44) sts.
Keeping motifs in line with lower part of sleeve, cont in patt as at beg, and AT THE SAME TIME dec one st at each end of every row until 16 sts rem, ending with a p row.
Cast/bind off 3 sts at beg of next 2 rows, then cast/bind off rem 10 sts.

NECKBAND
Join right shoulder seam.
With smaller needles, M and RS facing, pick up and k16 sts down Left Front neck, k front neck sts, pick up and k16 sts up Right Front neck and 4 sts down side of back neck, k back neck sts, then pick up and k5 sts up Left Back neck. 77 (83) sts.
Work in k1, p1 rib for 3 cm/1¼″.
Cast/bind off in rib.

ASSEMBLY
Press work according to in-structions on yarn band.
With crochet hook and M, work 2 rows of dc/sc along Left Back shoulder.
Work in same way on Right Front shoulder, making 3 button loops on 2nd row by working 2ch, miss/skip 1dc/sc.
Lap Left Front shoulder over back and stitch at armhole edge.
Sew in sleeves.
Join side and sleeve seams.
Press seams.
Sew on buttons.

Heather Suit

MATERIALS
Skirt:
3 50 g/1¾ oz balls (each approx 217 m/237 yds) of Patons *Beehive 4ply* (4 ply/fingering to sport weight yarn) in light shade (L)
2 balls in dark shade (D)
Cardigan:
3 balls in light shade (L)
2 balls in dark shade (D)
1 pair each of 2¾ mm/No 2 and 3¾ mm/No 5 needles
Shining elastic for skirt
2 buttons for skirt
7 buttons for cardigan

MEASUREMENTS
To fit approx 4–6 (6–8) years

Chest 61–66 (66–71) cm/24–26 (26–28)″

Skirt length (excluding waistband) 40 (45) cm/15¾ (17¾)″

Cardigan length 34 (39) cm/13½ (15½)″

Sleeve seam 27 (31) cm/10¾ (12¼)″

TENSION/GAUGE

28 sts and 36 rows to 10 cm/4″ over patt using 3¾ mm/No 5 needles.

SKIRT

BACK

With smaller needles and L, cast on 150 (157) sts and k4 rows.

Next row: K3 (7), *inc in next st, k11 (10), rep from * to last 3 (7) sts, inc in next st, k to end. 163 (171) sts.

Change to larger needles and cont in patt:

1st row: With L, k to end.
2nd row: With L, p to end.
3rd row: With D, k3, *keeping yarn at back of work, sl 1 purlwise, k3, rep from * to end.
4th row: With D, k3, *yarn to front of work – called yf, sl 1 purlwise, yarn to back of work – called ybk, k3, rep from * to end.
5th and 6th rows: As 1st and 2nd rows.
7th row: With D, k1, *sl 1 purlwise, k3, rep from * to last 2 sts, sl 1, k1.
8th row: With D, k1, *yf, sl 1, ybk, k3, rep from * to last 2 sts, yf, sl 1, ybk, k1.

Rep these 8 rows until work measures 40 (45) cm/15¾ (17¾)″ from beg, ending with a 1st or 5th row.

Break off D.

Next row: P0 (4), *p3 tog, [p2 tog, p1] twice, rep from * to last 1 (5) sts, p1 (5). 91 (99) sts.

Change to smaller needles.

Next row: K1, *p1, k1, rep from * to end.
Next row: P1, *k1, p1, rep from * to end.**

Rep last 2 rows 11 times more.

Cast/bind off in rib.

FRONT

Work as for Back to **, then rep last 2 rows 8 times more.

Next row: Rib 22 (24), cast/bind off 3 sts, rib to last 25 (27) sts, cast/bind off 3 sts, rib to end.

Next row: Rib to end, casting on 3 sts over each 3 cast/bound off.

Work 4 more rows in rib, then cast/bind off in rib.

STRAPS (make 2)

With smaller needles and L, cast on 11 sts and work in rib as for waist for 43 cm/17″ or length required.

Cast/bind off in rib.

ASSEMBLY

Do not press.
Join side seams.
Sew straps to top of back and sew a button to other end of each strap.
Pull in waist with shirring elastic.

CARDIGAN

BACK

With smaller needles and L, cast on 89 (97) sts and work in rib as for waistband for 4 cm/1½″, ending with a 2nd row and inc 6 sts evenly across last row. 95 (103) sts.

Change to larger needles and cont in patt as for Skirt until work measures 19 (22) cm/7½ (8¾)″ from beg, ending with a WS row.

Shape armholes

Cast/bind off 6 (7) sts at beg of next 2 rows.

Dec one st at each end of next 5 rows, then foll 3 (4) alt rows. 67 (71) sts.

Cont without shaping until armholes measure 15 (17) cm/6 (6¾)″, ending with a WS row.

Shape shoulders

Cast/bind off 6 sts at beg of next 4 rows, then 6 (7) sts at beg of next 2 rows.

Cast/bind off rem 31 (33) sts.

LEFT FRONT

With smaller needles and L, cast on 43 (47) sts and work in rib as for Back for 4 cm/1½″, ending with a 2nd row and inc 4 sts evenly across last row. 47 (51) sts.

Change to larger needles and cont in patt until work measures as for Back to armholes, ending with a WS row.

Shape armhole

Cast/bind off 6 (7) sts at beg of next row, then work 1 row.

Dec one st at armhole edge on next 5 rows, then on foll 3 (4) alt rows. 33 (35) sts.

Cont without shaping until

armhole measures 11 (12) cm/4¼ (4¾)″, ending with a RS row.

Shape neck

Cast/bind off 10 (11) sts at beg of next row, then dec one st at neck edge on next 5 rows.

Cont without shaping until armhole measures as for Back, ending with a WS row.

Shape shoulder

Cast/bind off 6 sts at beg of next and foll alt row.

Work 1 row.

Cast/bind off rem 6 (7) sts.

RIGHT FRONT

Work to match Left Front, reversing all shaping.

SLEEVES

With smaller needles and L, cast on 45 (47) sts and work in rib as for Back for 4 cm/1½″, ending with a 2nd row and inc 6 (8) sts evenly across last row.

Change to larger needles and cont in patt, inc one st at each end of 9th and every foll 4th (6th) row until there are 59 (61) sts, then on every 4th row until there are 75 (81) sts, working extra sts into patt.

Cont without shaping until sleeve measures 27 (31) cm/10¾ (12¼)″, ending with a WS row.

Shape top/cap

Cast/bind off 6 (7) sts at beg of next 2 rows.

Dec one st at each end of next and every alt row until 39 (41) sts rem, ending with a WS row.

Cast/bind off 2 sts at beg of next 4 rows.

Cast/bind off rem 31 (33) sts.

RUFFLE (make 2 pieces)

With smaller needles and D, cast on 239 (259) sts.

Break off D.

Join in L and p 1 row.

Next row: (RS) P3, *k1, p3, rep from * to end.

Next row: K3, *p1, k3, rep from * to end.

Rep last 2 rows for 5 cm/2″, ending with a WS row.

Next row: P3 tog, *k1, p3 tog, rep from * to end.

Cast/bind off loosely in rib.

NECKBAND

Join shoulder seams.

With smaller needles, L and RS facing, pick up and k75 (85) sts evenly around neck.

Beg with a 2nd row, work 8 rows in rib as for Back.
Cast/bind off in rib.

LEFT FRONT BORDER
With smaller needles and L, cast on 7 sts and work in rib as for Back until band fits up front edge (measured with band slightly stretched).
Cast/bind off.
Mark position of buttons, the first on 3rd row from beg, the 2nd on 4th row from top, then 5 more at equal intervals between these 2.

RIGHT FRONT BORDER
Work to match Left Front Border, making buttonholes at positions marked as foll:
1st buttonhole row: (RS facing) Rib 3, cast/bind off 2 sts, rib to end.
2nd buttonhole row: Rib 2, cast on 2 sts, rib to end.

ASSEMBLY
Do not press.
Sew in sleeves.
Join side and sleeve seams.
Sew on front borders.
Join 2 pieces of ruffle, then sew on ruffle with seam to Centre Back and catch sides of ruffle to front edges as in picture.
Sew on buttons.

Soft Buds

MATERIALS
- 4 (5) 50 g/$1\frac{3}{4}$ oz balls (each approx 220 m/240 yds) of Pingouin *Oued* (light weight mohair type)
- 1 pair each of $2\frac{3}{4}$ mm/No 2 and $3\frac{1}{4}$ mm/No 3 knitting needles
- $2\frac{3}{4}$ mm/No 2 and $3\frac{1}{4}$ mm/No 3 circular knitting needles
- 2.50 mm/size C crochet hook
- 7 small buttons

MEASUREMENTS
To fit approx 6–8 (8–10) years
Chest 66–71 (71–76) cm/26–28 (28–30)″
Length 48 (53) cm/$18\frac{3}{4}$ ($20\frac{3}{4}$)″
Sleeve seam 37 (41) cm/$14\frac{1}{2}$ ($16\frac{1}{4}$)″

TENSION/GAUGE
30 sts and 36 rows to 10 cm/4″ over patt using $3\frac{1}{4}$ mm/No 3 needles.

Note: Back and fronts are worked in one piece to armholes.

MAIN BODY
With smaller circular needle, cast on 199 (213) sts and work in k1, p1 rib for 5 cm/2″, ending with a RS row.
Next row: Rib 4 (1), *inc 1 by picking up loop between sts and work into back of loop, rib 10, rep from * to last 5 (2) sts, inc 1, rib to end. 219 (235) sts.
Change to larger circular needle and cont in patt as foll:
1st row: (RS) P5; *[k1, p1, k1, p1, k1] into next st, then pass 2nd, 3rd, 4th and 5th sts over first – called MB, p4, [k1, p2] twice, k1, p4, rep from * to last 6 sts, MB, p5.
2nd row: K5, *p1, k4, [p1, k2] twice, p1, k4, rep from * to last 6 sts, p1, k5.
3rd row: P5, *k1, p4, yon/yo, sl 1–k1–psso, p1, k1, p1, k2 tog, yrn/yo, p4, rep from * to last 6 sts, k1, p5.
4th row: K5, *p1, k5, [p1, k1] twice, p1, k5, rep from * to last 6 sts, p1, k5.
5th row: P2, *MB, p2, k1, p2, MB, p2, yon/yo, sl 1–k1–psso, k1, k2 tog, yrn/yo, p2, rep from * to last 9 sts, MB, p2, k1, p2, MB, p2.
6th row: K2, *[p1, k2] 3 times, k1, p3, k3, rep from * to last 9 sts, [p1, k2] 3 times.
7th row: *[P2, k1] 3 times, p3, yon/yo, sl 2 tog–k1–p2sso, yrn/yo, p1, rep from * to last 11 sts, p2, [k1, p2] 3 times.
8th row: [K2, p1] 3 times, *k9, [p1, k2] twice, p1, rep from * to last 2 sts, k2.
9th row: *[P2, k1] 3 times, p4, MB, p2, rep from * to last 11 sts, p2, [k1, p2] 3 times.
10th row: [K2, p1] 3 times, *k4, p1, k4, [p1, k2] twice, p1, rep from * to last 2 sts, k2.
11th row: *P2, yon/yo, sl 1–k1–psso, p1, k1, p1, k2 tog, yrn/yo, p4, k1, p2, rep from * to last 11 sts, p2, yon/yo, sl 1–k1–psso, p1, k1, p1, k2 tog, yon/yo, p2.
12th row: K3, *[p1, k1] twice, [p1, k5] twice, rep from * to last 8 sts, [p1, k1] 3 times, k2.
13th row: P3, *yon/yo, sl 1–k1–psso, k1, k2 tog, yrn/yo, p2, MB, p2, k1, p2, MB, p2, rep from * to last 8 sts, yon/yo, sl 1–k1–psso, k1, k2 tog, yrn/yo, p3.
14th row: K4, *p3, k3, [p1, k2] 3 times, k1, rep from * to last 7 sts, p3, k4.
15th row: P4, *yon/yo, sl 2 tog–k1–psso, yrn/yo, p3, [k1, p2] 3 times, p1, rep from * to last 7 sts, yon/yo, sl 2 tog–k1–p2sso, yrn/yo, p4.
16th row: K10, *[p1, k2] twice, p1, k9, rep from * to last st, k1.
These 16 rows form patt.
Cont in patt until work measures 32 (35) cm/$12\frac{1}{2}$ ($13\frac{3}{4}$)″ from beg, ending with a WS row.
Adjust length here if necessary.

Divide for armholes
Next row: Patt 50 (54), cast/bind off 10 sts, patt 99 (107) including st on needle, cast/bind off 10 sts, patt to end.
Cont on last 50 (54) sts for Left Front.
Cont without shaping until armhole measures 11 (13) cm/$4\frac{1}{2}$ (5)″, ending at front edge.

Shape neck
Cast/bind off 7 (8) sts at beg of next row, then dec one st at neck edge on every row until 30 (32) sts rem.
Cont without shaping until armhole measures 16 (18) cm/$6\frac{1}{4}$ (7)″, ending with a WS row.
Cast/bind off.
Return to next 99 (107) sts for Back and cont in patt until armhole measures as for Front, ending with a WS row.
Cast/bind off 30 (32) sts at beg of next 2 rows.
Cast/bind off rem 39 (43) sts.
Return to rem sts for Right Front and work to match Left Front, reversing shaping.

SLEEVES
With smaller needles, cast on 49 (55) sts and work in k1, p1 rib for 5 cm/2″, ending with a RS row.
Next row: Rib 4 (2), work twice into each of next 42 (52) sts, rib 3 (1).
Change to larger needles and cont in patt as on Main Body until sleeve measures 37 (41) cm/$14\frac{1}{2}$ ($16\frac{1}{4}$)″ from beg, ending with a WS row.
Adjust length here if required.
Place a marker at each end of last row, then work a further 6 rows.
Cast/bind off loosely.

ASSEMBLY
Join shoulder seams.
Join sleeve seams, leaving last 6 rows at top open.
Sew in sleeves, sewing the last 6 rows of sleeve seams to cast/bound-off sts at armholes.
With crochet hook and RS facing, work a row of dc/sc up Right Front edge, around neck and down Left Front, turn.
Work a 2nd row of dc/sc, making button loops on Right Front edge, the first 1 cm/$\frac{1}{2}$″ from neck edge, the last 1 cm/$\frac{1}{2}$″ from lower edge, then 5 more at equal intervals between.
To make button loop work 2ch, miss/skip 1dc/sc, 1dc/sc into next dc/sc.
Sew on buttons.

Sailor Suits

MATERIALS
Top:
- 3 (3, 4, 6, 7) 25 g/1 oz balls (each approx 112 m/122 yds) of Twilleys *Lyscordet* (light weight cotton) in main colour (M)
- 1 ball in contrast colour (C)

Skirt:

4 (5, 6, 7, 8) balls in main colour (M)

1 ball in contrast colour (C)

Shorts:

3 (3, 4, 5, 6) balls in main colour (M)

1 ball in contrast colour (C)

1 pair each of 2 mm/No 0 and 3 mm/No 3 knitting needles

4 buttons for top

Elastic for waist of skirt or shorts

MEASUREMENTS

To fit approx 1 (2, 4, 6, 8) years

Chest 51 (56, 61, 66, 71) cm/ 20 (22, 24, 26, 28)″

Length of top 28 (33, 38, 43, 48) cm/11 (13, 15, 16¾, 19)″

Sleeve seam 7 (8, 9, 10, 11) cm/2¾ (3¼, 3½, 4, 4¼)″

Length of skirt 28 (32, 46, 40, 44) cm/11 (12¾, 14¼, 15¾, 17¼)″

Length of shorts 30 (33, 36, 40, 44) cm/12 (13, 14¼, 15¾, 17½)″

TENSION/GAUGE

28 sts and 36 rows to 10 cm/ 4″ over st st using 3 mm/No 3 needles.

TOP

BACK

With smaller needles and M, cast on 77 (83, 91, 97, 105) sts and work in k1, p1 rib for 2 cm/¾″, ending with a WS row and inc one st in last row. 78 (84, 92, 98, 106) sts.

Change to larger needles and cont in st st until work measures 18 (22, 26, 30, 34) cm/7 (8¾, 10¼, 11¾, 13½)″, ending with a p row.

Shape armholes

Cast/bind off 4 sts at beg of next 2 rows, then dec one st at each end of next 7 (8, 10, 11, 13) rows. 56 (60, 64, 68, 72) sts.**

Cont without shaping until armholes measure 4 (5, 6, 7, 8) cm/1½ (2, 2½, 2¾, 3¼)″, ending with a p row.

Divide for opening

Next row: K26 (28, 30, 32, 34), turn and leave rem sts on spare needle.

Cont without shaping until armhole measures 10 (11, 12, 13, 14) cm/4 (4¼, 4¾, 5, 5½)″, ending with a p row.

Shape shoulders

Cast/bind off 6 sts at beg of

next and foll alt row, then 5 (6, 7, 8, 9) sts at beg of foll alt row.

Work 1 row, then cast/bind off rem 9 (10, 11, 12, 13) sts.

Return to sts on spare needle, rejoin yarn and cast/bind off 4 sts, k to end.

Cont to match first side.

FRONT

Work as for Back to **, then cont without shaping until armholes measure 6 (7, 8, 9, 10) cm/2½ (2¾, 3¼, 3½, 4)″, ending with a p row.

Shape neck

Next row: K23 (25, 27, 29, 31), turn and leave rem sts on spare needle.

Cast/bind off 3 sts at beg of next row, 2 sts at beg of next 1 (1, 2, 2, 2) alt rows, then dec one st at neck edge on every row until 17 (18, 19, 20, 21) sts rem.

Cont without shaping until armhole measures as for Back, ending at armhole edge.

Shape shoulder

Cast/bind off 6 sts at beg of next and foll alt row.

Work 1 row, then cast/bind off rem 5 (6, 7, 8, 9) sts.

Return to sts on spare needle, rejoin yarn and cast/bind off 10 sts, k to end.

Cont to match first side.

SLEEVES

With smaller needles and M, cast on 55 (59, 63, 67, 71) sts and work 4 rows in k1, p1 rib.

Change to larger needles and cont in st st, work [2 rows M, 4 rows C] twice, then cont in M until sleeve measures 7 (8, 9, 10, 11) cm/2¾ (3¼, 3½, 4, 4¼)″, ending with a p row.

Shape top/cap

Cast/bind off 4 sts at beg of next 2 rows.

Dec one st at each end of next 8 rows, then at each end of every alt row until 11 (13, 13, 15, 15) sts rem.

Cast/bind off.

COLLAR

With smaller needles and M, cast on 45 (50, 55, 60, 65) sts and work 8 rows in g st, inc 3 sts evenly across last row. 48 (53, 58, 63, 68) sts.

Change to larger needles and cont as foll:

1st row: K to end.

2nd row: K5, p to last 5 sts, k5.

Rep these 2 rows once more.

5th row: K8M, k in C to last 8 sts, k8M.

(**Note:** Use separate balls of each colour and twist colours where they join on every row.)

6th row: K5M, p3M, p in C to last 8 sts, p3M, k5M.

Rep last 2 rows once more.

9th row: K8M, 3C, k in M to last 11 sts, k3C, 8M.

10th row: K5M, p3M, 3C, p in M to last 11 sts, p3C, p3M, k5M.

Rep last 2 rows until work measures 6 (7, 8, 9, 10) cm/ 2½ (2¾, 3¼, 3½, 4)″, ending with a WS row.

Shape neck

Next row: Keeping colours correct, patt 19 (21, 23, 25, 27), turn and leave rem sts on spare needle.

Cast/bind off 3 sts at beg of next row, 2 sts at beg of foll 1 (1, 2, 2, 2) alt rows, then dec one st at neck edge on every row until 13 (14, 15, 16, 17) sts rem.

Cont without shaping until collar measures 10 (11, 12, 13, 14) cm/4 (4¼, 4¾, 5, 5½)″ from beg, ending with a RS row.

Place marker at beg of last row.

Next row: Cast on 10 (11, 12, 13, 14), patt to end.

Next row: Patt 13 (14, 15, 16, 17), then with M, k to end.

Next row: K5M, p5 (6, 7, 8, 9) M, patt to end.

Rep last 2 rows until back of collar measures as for Front from marker to stripe in C on Front, ending with a WS row.

Next row: K8M, k in C to last 5 sts, k5M.

Next row: K5M, p in C to last 8 sts, p3M, k5M.

Rep last 2 rows once more.

Break off C.

Next row: With M, k to end.

Next row: With M, k5, p to last 5 sts, k5.

Rep last 2 rows once more, dec 2 sts in last row.

Change to smaller needles and work 9 rows in g st.

Cast/bind off.

Return to sts on spare needle, with larger needles and M, cast/bind off centre 10 (11, 12, 13, 14) sts, patt to end.

Cont to match first side, reversing all shaping.

NECKBAND

Join shoulder seams.

With smaller needles and RS facing, pick up and k9 (10, 11, 12, 13) sts along Left Back neck, 19 (20, 21, 22, 23) sts down Left Front neck, 11 sts from front neck, 19 (20, 21, 22, 23) sts up Right Front neck, then 9 (10, 11, 12, 13) sts along Right Back neck. 67 (71, 75, 79, 83) sts.
Work 8 rows in k1, p1 rib.
Cast/bind off in rib.

BUTTONHOLE BORDER

With smaller needles and RS facing, pick up and k33 (35, 37, 39, 41) sts down right edge of back opening.
Work 3 rows in g st.
4th row: K3, *cast/bind off 2 sts, k6 (6, 7, 8, 8), rep from * twice more, cast/bind off 2 sts, k4 (6, 5, 4, 6).
5th row: K to end, casting on 2 sts over each 2 cast/bound off.
Work 3 more rows in g st.
Cast/bind off.

BUTTON BORDER

Work to match buttonhole border, omitting button-holes.

ASSEMBLY

Press work according to instructions on yarn band.
Sew in sleeves.
Join side and sleeve seams.
Sew down ends of borders at back.
Sew on collar.
Press seams.
Sew on buttons.

SKIRT

BACK

With smaller needles and M, cast on 71 (77, 83, 89, 95) sts and work 10 rows in k1, p1 rib.
Change to larger needles and cont in rib until work measures 8 cm/3¼", ending with a RS row.
Next row: P1 (3, 5, 7, 9), p twice into each of next 69 (71, 73, 75, 77) sts, p1 (3, 5, 7, 9). 140 (148, 156, 164, 172) sts.
Beg with a k row, cont in st st until work measures 23 (27, 31, 35, 39) cm/9 (10¾, 12¼, 13¾, 15¼)" from beg, or 5 cm/2" less than final length required, ending with a p row.
Work [4 rows in C, 2 rows in M] twice, dec 9 sts evenly across last row.
Change to smaller needles and work 9 rows in g st in M.

Cast/bind off.

FRONT

Work as for Back.

ASSEMBLY

Press work according to instructions on yarn band.
Join side seams.
Sew elastic to inside of waistband with a herringbone st casing.
Press seams.

SHORTS

BACK
Right leg

With smaller needles and M, cast on 41 (43, 47, 49, 53) sts.
Work 4 rows in k1, p1 rib, inc one st in last row on 2nd and 4th sizes. 41 (44, 47, 50, 53) sts.
Change to larger needles and work 4 rows in st st, join in C and work 4 rows in C, break off C and cont in M until work measures 14 (16, 18, 20, 22) cm/5½ (6¼, 7, 7¾, 8¾)", ending with a k row. Adjust length here if required.

Shape crotch
Cast/bind off 2 sts at beg of next row, then dec one st at beg of foll 3 alt rows, ending with a k row.
Break off yarn and leave sts on spare needle.

Left leg
Work as for Right Leg, reversing shaping at crotch and ending with a k row.

Join legs
Next row: P across sts of left leg to last st, p last st tog with first st of right leg, than p across rem sts of right leg. 71 (77, 83, 89, 95) sts.
Cont in st st until work measures 27 (30, 33, 37, 41) cm/10¾ (11¾, 13, 14½, 16¼)" from beg, or 3 cm/1¼" less than final length required, ending with a p row.

Shape back
1st and 2nd rows: Work to last 6 sts, turn.
3rd and 4th rows: Work to last 12 sts, turn.
Cont to work 6 sts less on every row 4 times more, then k across all sts.
Next row: P to end.
Change to smaller needles and work 10 rows in k1, p1 rib.
Cast/bind off in rib.

FRONT
Left leg
With smaller needles and M, cast on 39 (43, 45, 49, 51) sts.
Work 4 rows in k1, p1 rib, inc one st in last row on 1st, 3rd and 5th sizes. 40 (43, 46, 49, 52) sts.
Change to larger needles and work as for back of leg as far as crotch shaping, ending with a k row.

Shape crotch
Dec one st at beg of next and foll 3 alt rows, then work 1 row, ending with a k row.
Break off yarn and leave sts on spare needle.

Right leg
Work as for Left Leg, reversing shaping at crotch and ending with a k row.

Join legs
Join legs as for Back. 71 (77, 83, 89, 95) sts.
Cont as for Back, but omitting turning rows before rib.

ASSEMBLY

Press work according to instructions on yarn band.
Join side seams.
Join inside leg and crotch seams.
Sew elastic inside waist with a herringbone st casing.
Press seams.

Baby Togs

MATERIALS

4 (5) 50 g/1¾ oz balls (each approx 150 m/165 yds) of Pingouin *Pescadou/ Pingoperle* (light weight bouclé) in main colour (M)
3 (4) balls in 1st contrast colour (C)
1 ball in 2nd contrast colour (B)
1 pair each of 2¾ mm/No 2 and 3 mm/No 3 knitting

needles
5 buttons (3 in M and 2 in C)

MEASUREMENTS
To fit approx 8–12 (12–18) months
Chest 50 (55) cm/19¾ (21½)"
Length of pullover 28 (31) cm/11 (12¼)"
Sleeve seam 17 (19) cm/6¾ (7½)"
Trousers inside leg 27 (29) cm/10¾ (11½)"

TENSION/GAUGE
28 sts and 34 rows to 10 cm/4" over main patt using 3 mm/No 3 needles.

TROUSERS

RIGHT LEG
With smaller needles and M, cast on 54 (58) sts.
1st row: K2, *p2, k2, rep from * to end.
2nd row: P2, *k2, p2, rep from * to end.
Rep these 2 rows for 4 cm/1½", ending with a 1st row.
Next row: P2, [inc in each of next 3 sts, p1] 12 (13) times, inc in each of next 1 (2) sts, p3 (2). 91 (99) sts.
Change to larger needles and beg with a k row, work 6 rows in st st.
Work 13 rows of patt from chart I, reading chart from right to left for odd numbered rows and from left to right for even numbered rows.
Work 3 rows in M.
Work 11 rows of patt from chart II, then work 5 rows in M.
Cont in main patt as foll:
1st row: K1M, *1C, 7M, rep from * to last 2 sts, 1C, 1M.
2nd row: P1C, 1M, 1C, *5M, 1C, 1M, 1C, rep from * to end.
3rd–8th rows: Work 6 rows in M.
9th row: K5M, *1C, 7M, rep from * to last 6 sts, 1C, 5M.
10th row: P4M, *1C, 1M, 1C, 5M, rep from * to last 7 sts, 1C, 1M, 1C, 4M.
11th–16th rows: Work 6 rows in M.
These 16 rows form main patt and are rep throughout.
Cont in main patt until work measures 27 (29) cm/10¾ (11½)" from beg, ending with a p row.

Shape crotch
Cast/bind off 2 sts at beg of next 2 rows, then dec one st at each end of next and foll

alt row. 83 (91) sts.
Cont without shaping until work measures approx 41 (44) cm/16¼ (17¼)″ from beg, ending with a 6th or 14th row.
Work 11 rows of patt from chart II, then cont in M until work measures 45 (48) cm/17¾ (19)″ from beg, ending with a k row.
Next row: P4, *p2 tog, p4 (3), rep from * to last 7 sts, p2 tog, p5. 70 (74) sts.
Change to smaller needles and cont in rib as at beg for 8 cm/3¼″, ending with a WS row.**
Next row: Rib 14, cast/bind off 2 sts, rib to end.
Next row: Rib, casting on 2 sts over those cast/bound off. Work 2 more rows in rib, then cast/bind off loosely in rib.

LEFT LEG
Work as for Right Leg to **.
Next row: Rib to last 16 sts, cast/bind off 2 sts, rib to end.
Cont to match Right Leg.

STRAPS (make 2)
With smaller needles and M, cast on 6 sts and work in rib as for Right Leg for 40 (44) cm/15¾ (17¼)″ or length required. Cast/bind off in rib.

ASSEMBLY
Do not press.
Join back and front seams.
Join leg seams.
Sew one end of each strap to top of ribbing on back.
Sew a button to other end of each strap.

PULLOVER

BACK
With smaller needles and C, cast on 62 (70) sts and work 12 rows in rib as for Trousers, inc 7 sts evenly across last row. 69 (77) sts.
Change to larger needles and beg with a k row, work 6 rows in st st.
7th row: K2C, *1M, 7C, rep from * to last 3 sts, 1M, 2C.
8th row: P1C, *1M, 1C, 1M, 5C, rep from * to last 4 sts, [1M, 1C] twice.
9th–14th rows: Work 6 rows in M.
15th row: K6C, *1M, 7C, rep from * to last 7 sts, 1M, 6C.
16th row: P5C, *1M, 1C, 1M, 5C, rep from * to end.
These 16 rows form patt.
Cont in patt until work measures 18 (20) cm/7 (7¾)″ from beg, ending with a p row.

Shape armholes
Cast/bind off 4 sts at beg of next 2 rows. 61 (69) sts.
Cont without shaping until work measures 28 (31) cm/11 (12¼)″ from beg, ending with a p row.

Shape shoulders and neck
Next row: Cast/bind off 8 (9), k until there are 17 (19) sts on RH needle, turn and leave rem sts on spare needle.
Next row: Cast/bind off 9, p to end.
Cast/bind off rem 8 (10) sts.
Return to sts on spare needle, sl first 11 (13) sts on to st holder, rejoin yarn and k to end.
Cont to match first side.

FRONT
Work as for Back until 14 rows less than Back to shoulders.

Shape neck
Next row: K25 (28), turn and leave rem sts on spare needle.
Cast/bind off 3 sts at beg of next row, 2 sts at beg of foll 2 alt rows, then one st at beg of foll 2 alt rows. 16 (19) sts.
Cont without shaping until work measures as for Back to shoulders, ending with a p row.

Shape shoulder
Cast/bind off 8 (9) sts at beg of next row.
P 1 row, then cast/bind off rem 8 (10) sts.
Return to sts on spare needle, sl first 11 (13) sts on to st holder for neck, rejoin yarn and k to end.
Cont to match first side.

SLEEVES
With smaller needles and C, cast on 38 (42) sts and work 12 rows in rib as for Trousers, inc 9 (11) sts evenly across last row. 47 (53) sts.
Change to larger needles and beg with a k row, work 6 rows in st st.
7th row: K3 (2) C, *1M, 7C, rep from * to last 4 (3) sts, 1M, 3 (2) C.
This sets position of patt.
Cont in patt, inc one st at each end of next and every foll 8th row until there are 55 (61) sts, working extra sts into patt.
Cont without shaping until sleeve measures 17 (19) cm/6¾ (7½)″ from beg, ending with a p row.
Place a marker at each end of last row, then work 6 rows. Cast/bind off loosely.

SHOULDER BORDER
With smaller needles, C and RS facing, pick up and k17 (20) sts along Left Front shoulder. Work 2 rows in g st.
Next row: K8 (9), cast/bind off 2 sts, k to end.
Next row: K7 (9), cast on 2 sts, k to end.
Work 2 more rows, then cast/bind off.
Work along Left Back shoulder in same way, omitting buttonhole.

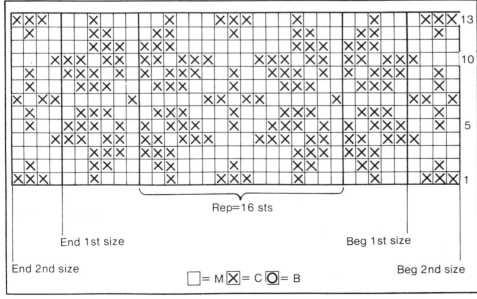

Rep=16 sts

End 1st size

End 2nd size

Beg 1st size

Beg 2nd size

☐ = M ☒ = C ⊡ = B

Chart I for making Baby Togs

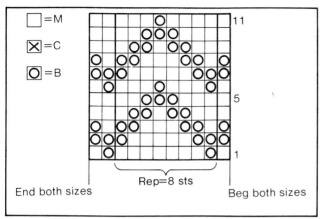

Key:
□ = M
⊠ = C
◯ = B

11

5

1

Rep = 8 sts

End both sizes

Beg both sizes

Chart II for making Baby Togs

NECKBAND

Join right shoulder seam. With smaller needles, C and RS facing, pick up and k53 (55) sts around front neck including sts on st holder, then 33 (35) sts across back neck. 86 (90) sts.
Beg with a 2nd row, work 3 rows in rib as for Trousers.
Next row: Rib 2, cast/bind off 2, rib to end.
Next row: Rib to end, casting on 2 sts over those cast/bound off.
Work 2 more rows, in rib, then cast/bind off in rib.

ASSEMBLY

Do not press.
Lap Left Front shoulder over back and stitch at armhole edge.
Sew in sleeves, sewing the last 6 rows of sleeve seams to cast/bound-off sts at armholes.
Join side and sleeve seams.
Sew on buttons.

HAT

With smaller needles and C, cast on 90 sts and work 6 rows in rib as for Trousers, inc 3 sts evenly across last row. 93 sts.
Change to larger needles and beg with a k row, cont in patt as for pullover until work measures 12 (13) cm/4¾ (5)" from beg, ending with a p row.

Shape top

Cast/bind off 32 sts at beg of next 2 rows, then cont in patt on rem 29 sts, dec one st at each end of every 10th row until 23 sts rem, then cont without shaping until edge of this piece measures same as cast/bound-off sts, ending with a p row.

Break off yarn and leave sts on st holder.
Join side edges of this piece to cast/bound-off edges.

Face edge

With smaller needles and M, cast on 32 sts and with same needle pick up and k32 (34) sts up right side of face; k across sts on st holder, knitting 2 tog in centre, pick up and k32 (34) sts down left side of face. 118 (122) sts.
Work 2 rows in rib as for Trousers.
Next row: Rib to last 4 sts, cast/bind off 2 sts, rib to end.
Next row: Rib 2, cast on 2 sts, rib to end.
Work 2 more rows in rib, then cast/bind off in rib.

ASSEMBLY

Sew button to Left Front neck to correspond with buttonhole.

Palm Tree

MATERIALS

4 (5) 50 g/1¾ oz balls (each approx 238 m/260 yds) of Sirdar *Country Style 4-ply*

(4 ply/fingering to sport weight yarn) in main colour (A)
1 ball in each of 8 contrasting colours (B, C, D, E, F, G, H and I)
1 pair each of 2¾ mm/No 2 and 3¼ mm/No 3 knitting needles
2.50 mm/size C crochet hook
4 small buttons

MEASUREMENTS

To fit 56 (61) cm/22 (24)" chest
Length 32 (39) cm/12½ (15¼)"
Sleeve seam 20 (25) cm/7¾ (9¾)"

TENSION/GAUGE

28 sts and 36 rows to 10 cm/4" over st st using 3¼ mm/No 3 needles.

FRONT

With smaller needles and B, cast on 86 (92) sts.
1st row: *K2, p2, rep from * to last 2 sts, k2.
2nd row: P2, *k2, p2, rep from * to end.
Rep these 2 rows 4 (5) times more, inc 1st in last row. 87 (93) sts.
Change to larger needles. Beg with a k row and working in st st throughout, work in colour patt from chart, reading odd numbered rows from right to left and even rows from left to right, until 96 (102) rows have been worked, so ending with a p row.

Shape neck

Cont in patt, k36 (38), turn leaving rem sts on spare needle.
Dec one st at neck edge on next 7 rows. 29 (31) sts.
Work 6 (8) rows without shaping, so ending with a p row.

Shape shoulder

Cast/bind off 15 (16) sts at beg of next row.
Work 1 row.
Cast/bind off rem 14 (15) sts.
With RS of work facing, sl centre 15 (17) sts on to st holder and rejoin yarn to rem 36 (38) sts and k to end.
Complete to match first side reversing shaping.

BACK

Work as for Front until 110 (118) rows have been worked from chart, omitting palm tree, dolphin and sun, and

neck shaping.
Shape shoulders
Cast/bind off 15 (16) sts at beg of next 2 rows, then 14 (15) at beg of next 2 rows.
Leave rem 29 (31) sts on spare needle.

SLEEVES

With smaller needles and B, cast on 42 (46) sts.
1st row: *K2, p2, rep from * to last 2 sts, k2.
2nd row: P2, *k2, p2, rep from * to end.
Rep these 2 rows 4 (6) times more.
Next row: Rib 1 (3), inc 1 st, [rib 8, inc 1 st] 5 times, rib 1 (3). 48 (52) sts.
Change to larger needles. Beg with a k row, work in st st, inc one st at each end of next and every foll 6th row until there are 68 (76) sts.
Cont without shaping until sleeve seam measures 20 (25) cm/7¾ (9¾)", ending with a p row.
Cast/bind off.

ASSEMBLY

Join right shoulder seam.
With smaller needles, B, and right side facing, pick up and k17 sts down left side of neck edge, k15 (17) sts from Centre Front, pick up and k17 sts up right side of neck edge and finally k centre 29 (31) sts from back. 78 (82) sts.
Cast/bind off in rib.
Join 2.5 cm/1" of left shoulder seam from armhole edge.
Place centre of cast/bound-off edge of sleeves to shoulder seams and sew sleeves to front and back.
Join side and sleeve seams.
With crochet hook and B, and right side of work facing, beg at top of neck border on back and work one row of dc/sc all around opening, making 4 button loops on front edge, the first 1 cm/½" from seam, the last at neck edge and the rem 2 spaced equally between. To make button loop work 7ch, miss/skip one st, 1dc/sc in next st. Fasten off. Sew on buttons.

107

Decorative Techniques

Two basic crochet stitches and swiss darning/duplicate stitching are used to trim and decorate several of the patterns in this book.

Crochet

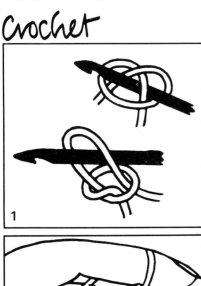

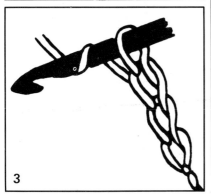

Foundation Chain *Ch*
Make a slip knot about 15 cm/6″ from end of yarn (1).

Holding hook in right hand and yarn in left, wind yarn anticlockwise round hook (2), and draw yarn through slip knot to make one chain.

The working loop on the hook never counts as a stitch.

Continue (3). Move left hand along chain to hold the previous stitch.

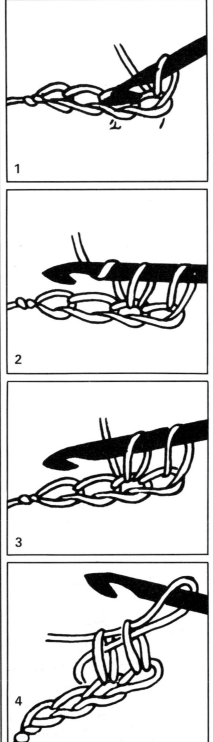

Double Crochet (UK) *dc*
Single Crochet (USA) *sc*
Insert hook from front to back into 2nd chain from hook (1), draw up a loop and wind yarn round hook (2). Draw yarn through stitch. There are now 2 loops on hook (3).

Wind yarn once round hook again and draw yarn through both loops on hook (4).

Repeat along chain. Turn work so that last stitch becomes first stitch of next row.

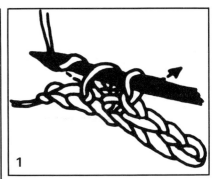

Slip Stitch *ss/sl st*
Insert hook from front to back into 2nd chain from hook and wind yarn once round hook, as for dc/sc. Draw yarn through both chain and loop (1) on hook, leaving one loop on hook.

Embroidery

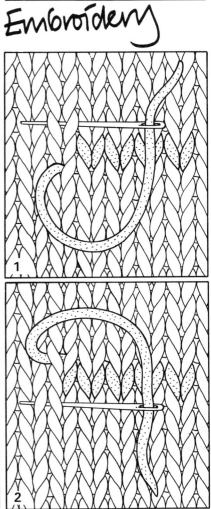

Swiss Embroidery/Duplicate Stitch. This is a method of embroidering a Fairisle effect or coloured pattern on a stocking stitch base by retracing the path of the original stitch. It is worked from right to left. Figs. 1 and 2.
Cross stitch is worked by simply making two overlapping stitches, as shown on page 45.

Yarn Suppliers

NB: The patterns in this book give the brand name of the yarn each garment has been made up in. The distributors of these yarns are listed below. But the life of a book and the availability of a particular yarn are not always the same. A book generally lasts much longer. Moreover, yarns that are easy to get in one place are difficult to find in another. Therefore, in addition to brand names, each yarn also has a generic name based on fibre and weight. Readers who wish to substitute an equivalent yarn for a brand name should take note of each skein length and pay special attention to information in the introduction about tension and yarn substitution.

Argyll

Argyll Wools Ltd
Priestly Mills
Pudsey
W. Yorkshire
England

Estelle Designs
221 Broadview
Toronto
Canada

Lister–Lee

George Lee & Sons Ltd.
Whiteoak Mills
P.O. Box 37
Wakefield
W. Yorkshire
England

J. H. Imports Ltd
P.O. Box 326
Millersville
Maryland 21108
USA

Anita Hurtig Imports Ltd
5726 Burleigh Crescent
Calgary, Alberta T2H108
Canada

Patons & Jaeger

Patons & Baldwin Ltd
MacMullen Road
Darlington
Co. Durham DL1 1YQ
England

Susan Bates Inc.
212 Middlesex Avenue
Chester
Connecticut 06412
USA

Patons & Baldwin Canada
Inc
1001 Roselawn Avenue
Toronto, Ontario MbB1B8
Canada

Phildar

Phildar UK Ltd
4 Gambrel Road
Westgate Industrial Estate
Northampton NN5 5NF
England

Phildar Inc
6438 Dawson Boulevard
85 North
Norcroft
Georgia 300093
USA

Phildar Ltee
6200 Est
Boulevard H. Bouraffa
Montreal Nord H1G 5X3
Canada

Pingouin

French Wools Ltd
7–11 Lexington Street
London W1R 4BU
England

Pingouin Yarns
P.O. Box 100
Highway 45
Jameston
South Carolina 29453
USA

Promafil Limitee
1500 Rue Jules Poitras
379 St Laurent
Quebec H4N-1X7
Canada

Robin

Robin Mills
Idle
Bradford
W. Yorkshire
England

Plymouth Yarn Co.
P.O. Box 28
500 Lafayette Street
Bristol
Pennsylvania 19007
USA

S. R. Kertzer Ltd
257 Adelaide Street W.
Toronto, Ontario M5H 1Y1
Canada

Sirdar

Sirdar PLC
Flanshaw Lane
Alverthorpe
Wakefield
W. Yorkshire WF2 9ND
England

Kendex Corporation
31332 Via Colinas 107
Westlake Village
California 91362
USA

Diamond Yarns (Canada)
Corp.
153 Bridgeland Avenue,
Unit 11
Toronto, Ontario M6A 2Y6
Canada

Twilleys

H. G. Twilley Ltd
Roman Mill
Stamford
Lincolnshire P/9 1BG
England

House of Settler
2120 Broadway
Lubbock, Texas 79401
USA

Leon Summers
456 South Norton Avenue
Los Angeles
California 90020

S. R. Kertzer Ltd
257 Adelaide Street W.
Toronto, Ontario M5H 1Y1
Canada

List of Patterns

Acknowledgments

Illustrations by
    Coral Mula – colour charts and how to knit
    diagrams
    Catherine Ward – fashion sketches, pages
    50 and 17
    Nicola Spoor – page 38
    Hilly Beavan – page 42

Many thanks to Benetton, French Connection,
Harvey Nichols and Liberty for the clothes and
accessories: Start-rite for the children's shoes; C
& N, 5 Dryden Street, London WC2 for the
perspex jewellery and buttons. The Button Box,
44 Bedford Street, London WC2 and J. T.
Morgan, 28 Chepstow Place, London WC4;
Paperchase, Tottenham Court Road, London W1.

Gabi Tubbs would also like to thank the yarn
manufacturers and their press officers, friends
and family who were involved in producing this
book and gave tremendous support.

Knitting design on title page is by Michael
Ross, whose designs are available at Libertys.